Healing Kundalini Symptoms

Proven Techniques that Really Work

Tara Springett

ISBN: 9781689344975

Contents

Acknowledgements

Firstly, I want to thank all my clients who have worked with me. I learned more about the kundalini process from each one of you.

Many thanks also to my dear husband Nigel who has actively supported me with this project, just as he did with all my other books. I am thankful that he has also allowed me to assist and advise him in his kundalini process. And I am particularly pleased that he has now trained with me as a kundalini therapist and that we now work together in our kundalini therapy practice to help with the great flood of clients from all over the world.

I thank all my spiritual and psychotherapeutic teachers: Victor Chu, Roland Kopp-Wichmann, Phyllis Crystal, Willi Trienen, Shenpen Hookham, Rigdzin Shikpo, His Eminence Garchen Rinpoche and especially I thank my inner gurus Anandamayi Ma and White Tara.

Introduction

In this book, I will introduce simple methods that have helped over a thousand of my clients with kundalini symptoms quickly and effectively. My clients often suffered from the most extreme problems but were usually liberated from their pain, fears, strong emotions and confusion by the methods described in this book within weeks or a few months. They now experience the kundalini process as a gift and living happy and meaningful lives.

It is the promise of this book that everyone who seriously uses the methods within it can expect a significant improvement in their kundalini symptoms or even complete elimination of them. Not only that - the kundalini is, in essence, an expansion of consciousness and as soon the first difficult symptoms subside, you can expect to experience more creativity, more joyful feelings, deeper spiritual wisdom and in some cases even supernatural powers such as clairvoyance or spiritual healing.

My own kundalini was awakened over 40 years ago at the tender age of 17 and became more clearly apparent at the age of 24. Therefore, I spent all of my adult life with this phenomenon. When I was young, there was no Internet and I first heard of the term kundalini at the age of 28 when my Buddhist teacher read from the books of Gopi Krishna. The experiences of Gopi Krishna, however, were so extreme that I did not recognise myself in them.

I only truly understood what was going on with me when I asked my Buddhist teacher Garchen Rinpoche for the tummo transmission at the age of 40. Tummo is the Tibetan Buddhist equivalent of kundalini awakening as described in Lama Yeshe's book *Bliss of Inner Fire: Heart Practice of the Six Yogas of Naropa*. Unfortunately, I had difficulties with the tummo practice and therefore began to read all sorts of books on the subject and it was only then that I realised I had been in the kundalini process almost all my life!

By that time, I had already been a psychotherapist for many years and had also received permission to teach meditation and Buddhist philosophy from two Buddhist teachers. I had conducted thousands of psychotherapy sessions and had guided meditation groups for many years. So, it seemed a good idea to share my knowledge with clients who also suffered from kundalini symptoms. I created a website in 2010 and started to work with kundalini clients from all around the world. At first, the clients trickled in but they increased with each passing year until I was literally flooded with people who were more or less desperate to receive my help. For that reason, I have decided to describe in this book how I help people to liberate themselves quickly and effectively from all their kundalini symptoms.

This book also addresses therapists and psychiatrists who want to know more about this phenomenon, which is sometimes described in the psychiatric literature as a "spiritual crisis". To heal such a crisis, it is firstly important to understand thoroughly what constitutes the kundalini phenomenon and, secondly, to know how to apply the method of higher-consciousness healing.

Higher-consciousness healing is a transpersonal healing modality that I developed approximately 20 years ago. "Transpersonal" means that it combines spirituality with psychology. The method consists of effective Tibetan Buddhist techniques - presented in a simple way – that will heal all the afflictions that can occur in the kundalini process. Higher-consciousness healing uses simple visualisation and breathing techniques but it is not important to be good at visualising. It is enough to feel the things to be visualised are there or to simply "perceive" them just like a playing child would. I have described the general method in detail in my book *The Five-Minute Miracle*. Here, in this book, I will describe this healing technique again and how to apply it to kundalini symptoms.

In 2014, I published my first book about kundalini *Enlightenment Through the Path of Kundalini*. It deals mainly with the questions of how to awaken the kundalini and how to use it to reach spiritual enlightenment. If you want to know more about my personal story, you can read it there. In this book, I will mostly talk about how to overcome any painful, confusing or frightening kundalini symptoms most quickly and effectively.

A kundalini awakening is a very mysterious phenomenon but I have tried my best to give down-to-earth, practical advice that people of all faiths can follow and I hope my guidelines will also be understood and accepted by psychotherapists and health practitioners with a more Western outlook. Everything described in this book is based on the experience I have gained from treating over a thousand clients in many thousands of therapy sessions. Only if there was no other way to explain certain concepts, have I referred to the spiritual wealth of Tibetan Buddhism.

Unfortunately, there is very little practical knowledge for the treatment of kundalini crises from other psychotherapists or spiritual teachers. Even Tibetan Buddhist teachers usually have little to say about the so-called *lung*-diseases (literally translated "wind-diseases" which means "energy-diseases" and are the Tibetan Buddhist equivalents of kundalini symptoms). They often content themselves with the advice of reducing spiritual practice, drinking some alcohol and eating more meat. Among Western therapists, I did not find much useful information either about how to deal with a sudden opening of the subconscious mind and the many symptoms that accompany this process. Most therapists only give general advice and, unfortunately, often use methods that have been developed for people without kundalini syndrome. Their techniques therefore often do not help or can even cause damage.

Due to this lack of expertise among Eastern and Western therapists and spiritual teachers, I see myself as a researcher and even pioneer in the field of the treatment of spiritual crises. I have learned from each of my clients what works and what does not and over the years refined, improved and expanded my methods. The result of this work you now hold in your hands and I will explain everything in detail without holding anything back. It is my hope that many sufferers will learn to help themselves through this book and that therapists and psychiatrists, too, will gain knowledge of how to help their clients with kundalini symptoms more effectively.

I want to reassure all my readers right from the start that my clients have had extremely good results with the methods outlined in this book and there are many testimonials on the www.taraspringett.com and www.kundalinisymptoms.com websites that confirm this point.

Chapter one
What is Kundalini?

At this point, I could have written about deep philosophical and spiritual theories, but as promised, I have restricted myself to the down-to-earth descriptions that I observed directly with my clients and myself.

Kundalini is expanded consciousness

The best way to understand the kundalini phenomenon is to imagine it as expanded consciousness. This means that we perceive more clearly and more intensely what is going on in our own mind and around us. Our consciousness expands in four principal areas:

Opening of our subconscious mind
Perception of (hidden) mental content in other people
Paranormal experiences
Spiritual experiences

In the following sections we will be looking at these four areas more closely:

Things that were subconscious now become conscious: These may be old memories coming to the surface, uncomfortable feelings that we normally suppress or impulses that we would call anti-social. Also, our sense perceptions such as sounds, smells and taste can be greatly intensified, which can be very uncomfortable so that situations we could tolerate before become almost painful (e.g. going to the shopping centre or listening to the news). Fortunately, agreeable sense perceptions are amplified too and these can lead to a lot of joy and even bliss (e.g. the sight of beautiful nature).

The opening of the unconscious mind can also lead to all sorts of physical symptoms such as internal heat, pressure feelings, ascending energies and pain without a medical reason. All these symptoms consist of our emotions that are arising from our unconscious mind but which we have not yet recognised as such. I will explain more about this dynamic later.

For many people, the opening of the unconscious mind causes anxiety in the initial phase, firstly, through the intensification of all our emotions and, secondly, through the fear *about* all these strange changes. However, it is important to understand that the kundalini process does not add any new mental or emotional content into our being but only intensifies what has been within us all along.

It is of course not always easy to deal with this previously repressed material and in this book, I will explain in detail how to calm down our sometimes highly dramatic feelings and how to deal with traumatic memories that may come up. I will also explain how we can learn to perceive the emotions within our physical symptoms and then dissolve them with higher-consciousness healing.

Hidden motivations and feelings of other people become accessible: Many people wear a mask in their daily interactions and pretend to be someone other than who they really are. This is especially true for the selfish impulses and aggression that many people try to keep secret as well as "embarrassing" emotions such as envy, greed, depression, anxiety and inappropriate sexual impulses. Through the expanded awareness in the kundalini process, these feelings, intentions and impulses in others become more perceptible to us.

This new knowledge about others can certainly be an advantage because it enables us to assess whether we can trust other people, improve our relationships with them and help them more effectively. However, sometimes what we see in others leads to disappointment and confusion because we have to learn that people are not always as nice as they seemed to be. Old friendships and relationships with family members often need to be changed and sometimes even terminated. Often, my clients have problems with people who have personality disorder traits and whose selfishness they can no longer tolerate even if they endured their behaviour for many years. Later, I will go into detail about how our relationships change after a kundalini awakening and how we can actively improve them.

Paranormal Phenomena: Everyone in the kundalini process will sooner or later get experiences that can be described as paranormal or supernatural. These are things like telepathy, spiritual healing, visions of ghosts, demons and divine beings, contact with the dead, clairvoyance and extremely unlikely coincidences. Some people are also in contact with extra-terrestrials, see things like balls of light, hear strange sounds or voices or leave their bodies - all things that are not supposed to happen from our normal, rational worldview.

These experiences are by no means forms of psychosis because people in the kundalini process are usually completely aware that these phenomena are commonly considered as not "normal" and can entertain a reasonable measure of doubt about what they experienced. They are also able to talk about these experiences (which people with real mental illness usually cannot do). It is precisely this awareness that is the sign of their mental health. In other words, paranormal experiences during the kundalini process add another dimension to our normal understanding of the world, while mentally ill people lose our normal view of the world.

It is easy to see, of course, that the world of the paranormal can cause many fears and confusions and I will provide a thorough guide of how to deal confidently with such phenomena. I will also show how paranormal experiences can be controlled so that we only have positive experiences that can be used for things like spiritual healing, channelling or for counselling.

Spiritual experiences: The true and ultimate purpose of a kundalini awakening is to experience higher spiritual states of mind and stabilize these experiences. Without kundalini, we can pray and meditate for many years without ever having meaningful spiritual experiences. Only through the expanded consciousness of the kundalini process is it possible to fill one's mind with divine bliss, experience deep states of all-embracing love or have profound experiences of union with a divine being.

The block of ice metaphor

To illustrate the kundalini process, I like to use the image of a block of ice that melts into water and then evaporates into steam. In this image, the ice-block represents our repressed feelings and unconscious material that we cannot yet access. In other words, before a kundalini awakening our energy body (or emotional body) is frozen into ice, we are numb and rigid, we feel very little and we change only minimally in the course of our lives.

Through a kundalini awakening, the ice begins to melt and transforms into water. The water represents our suppressed emotions, which now begin to flow freely. Also, the thoughts and beliefs that generated the emotions are released into our consciousness. Some of these emotions belong to repressed traumas while other feelings and beliefs are just childish, irrational or inappropriate and it requires some psychological work to sort all these emotions out, calm them down and finally dissolve them.

Through the melting of the ice, we also become very sensitive because everything that touches the water penetrates deeply into it and no longer bounces off its surface as was the case with the block of ice. Therefore, we often feel more easily hurt by small digs and manipulations of other people and can no longer ignore these things as easily as before. On the other hand, a prayer or the sight of untouched nature can provoke profound states of bliss. We also become more sensitive towards all sensations like noises, smells, sights or "atmospheres" and "vibrations".

Many of my clients feel that this part of the kundalini process is more or less a disaster because they want to stay as strong and thick-skinned as they were before. But it is important to look at this melting process as something positive because it enables us to clean out our unprocessed psychological complexes, negative attitudes and repressed traumas from our unconscious mind. It is only through this inner healing that we become able to come closer to the divine and ultimately reach enlightenment. In our block of ice metaphor, enlightenment means that the water now starts to evaporate and transforms into steam. Once this happens, our negative emotions transform into bliss and ecstatic

13

rapture accompanied by deep spiritual insight and wisdom.

All this is not just a nice theory. I myself experience these states of bliss virtually every day - often for many hours - and I have also taught many of my clients to experience the same. In this book, I will show you how to use inner alchemy to transform ice into water - that is, transform numbness and pain into emotions and then dissolve all negative emotions with higher-consciousness healing. People who would then like to learn to transform water into steam and reach states of spiritual bliss should read my books *Spiritual Joy* and *Enlightenment Through the Path of Kundalini*. It is easier to accomplish this than most people imagine.

If we look at the block of ice metaphor, we can see that during the kundalini process nothing new has been added to our being. All the strange symptoms, all the extreme feelings and all the other amazing or terrifying phenomena are always just the same "material" (water) - just in different states or aggregates. When we feel nothing, we are in the state of ice; when we have strong feelings, we are in the state of water; when we experience spiritual bliss, we are in the state of steam.

Physical symptoms, such as shaking, twitching, pain and involuntary movements are, according to our metaphor, lumps of ice swirling around in the wild stream of our emotions and bashing or rubbing up against each other in an unpleasant way. These physical symptoms represent semi-repressed psychological material or emotions that have not been recognised as such. It is this half-conscious material that causes all the unpleasant "energy phenomena" in our bodies. Once these ice chunks (the repressed feelings) melt (become conscious), the physical symptoms often vanish virtually overnight.

I have conducted this process of transformation in many hundreds of therapy sessions, much to the astonishment of my clients who were often afraid that they had been physically damaged by the kundalini process. I can already now reassure all readers who are afraid of physical injuries that in all the years that I have been working as a kundalini therapist, I have not seen a single case in which the kundalini process has caused any physical damage at all.

In the image of the block of ice, we can also recognise that the kundalini

14

energy itself is neutral. It melts the ice (the unconscious mind) but it does not determine the contents (the emotions) that emerge from the ice. For this reason, statements such as, "The kundalini was very painful today", make no sense. One should rather say, "Today, some material emerged from my subconscious mind that I could not recognise as an emotion and therefore perceived as pain."

The kundalini itself never causes pain - it is only our attitudes that lead to problems. For example, it is difficult for many of us to admit that we carry primitive emotions such as greed, envy, and sadistic aggression within us because these emotions do not match the often overly positive image that we might have of ourselves. For the kundalini process to work smoothly and harmoniously, it is necessary to be as humble and honest as possible. I will show in this book how we can eliminate and heal all kundalini symptoms — without exception - through this courageous process of becoming ever more self-aware.

The block of ice metaphor also explains how a kundalini awakening comes about in the first place: It is the "burning" desire to transform ourselves and expand our consciousness that motivates people to participate in challenging exercises - such as a ten-day silent meditation retreat - and thus generate the necessary "heat" that causes our frozen energy body to melt. The kundalini process (the melting of the ice) is therefore accelerated by spiritual devotion and deep relaxation in prayer and meditation. Once this process is underway and the ice has turned into a raging stream of water, it is therefore not very wise to simply surrender to it as this would make the water flow even more wildly. What we need at this stage are skilful methods to control and heal our intense emotions. In our picture, this means that we learn to stabilise the banks of our water stream and canalise the water (our emotions) in positive ways. This happens of course through the practice of higher-consciousness healing. The most talented people can also immediately begin to evaporate the water, which means turning their negative emotions into bliss.

The puberty metaphor

A second metaphor that explains the kundalini process very well is puberty. During puberty, a new dimension opens up which was already within us as a seed. It is the same in the kundalini process: at a certain time, a pre-existing force opens up within us and changes us completely - just like children completely change when they go through puberty.

Most children nowadays are well-prepared for adolescence and know what puberty is all about through watching television and by observing their environment. So in most cases, they can handle it fairly well. However, imagine that you are the only child that goes through puberty and that no one has prepared you for it. Understandably, you would become quite scared and believe that you are suffering from some serious illness. This is exactly the situation in which many of my kundalini clients find themselves.

It is, therefore, one of my most important tasks as a kundalini therapist to explain to my clients that they are not suffering from a disease but are undergoing an expansion of consciousness in a process that has many similarities with puberty. Both developments open up dimensions in us that we may have heard of before but have never experienced within ourselves. The developments are not dangerous, we are not crazy and we do not need to be cured. All we need is some help to deal with the material that arises from our subconscious mind and, in some cases, from the paranormal world. It is also important to understand that this process - just like puberty - cannot be reversed and is a positive development when it is recognised for what it is.

The dimension that opens up during puberty is sexuality and the main dimension that opens up during a kundalini awakening is spirituality. I have had many clients who, before their kundalini awakening, did not want to have anything to do with religion or spirituality and then suddenly became extremely interested in the subject and began to change their entire lives accordingly. In religious literature, such a development is often called a "conversion experience" and usually causes surprise, incomprehension and, unfortunately, often resistance from family members. Therefore, in many cases, it requires a lot of patience and skilful communication to integrate such an awakening into our partnership and our entire life.

As a word of warning, I also want to point out that the kundalini process can be abused - just like sexuality can be used to cause harm. If we misuse paranormal experiences and supernatural powers for selfish purposes then this process can cause terrible suffering. Many "successful" charlatans and cult leaders who seduce and exploit their naïve and gullible followers with magic and false spirituality are people with awakened but corrupted kundalini.

We should keep this warning in mind because, unfortunately, there are many misleading statements that the kundalini process is a guaranteed and direct path to enlightenment. This is just as untrue as saying that puberty is the direct and guaranteed route to a happy family life. In both cases, the original awakening is the prerequisite for a higher development but it is by no means a certainty.

To use the kundalini energy for enlightenment requires a deep inner commitment to abide by ethical rules and an honest desire to make love the centrepiece of one's life. Interestingly, this applies equally to the development of a happy family life. In both processes, we can easily lose our way and it takes a lot of patience and constant practise to achieve either goal.

Even though the kundalini energy can be misused for evil purposes, its primary impact on people is fundamentally beneficial and positive - just like puberty is. Both processes are neither diseases nor mental disorders. Just as puberty is a prerequisite for falling in love, having a loving sexuality and a happy family, so a kundalini awakening is a prerequisite for the highest spiritual joys and realisations.

Energy channels, chakras and blockages

In many books that come from Tibetan Buddhism, Taoism or Kundalini Yoga, we can find beautiful pictures in which the kundalini energy flows in an orderly way through energy channels and points in the body (chakras). The best-known energy channel comes from the Hindu system and is called the sushumna. It runs through the middle of the body from the perineum to the crown and is flanked by two other channels, the ida and pingala, which cross over at each chakra. According to the Hindu system, there are seven chakras: in the genitals, lower abdomen, navel, heart, neck, forehead and crown of the head. In the Tibetan system, there are only five chakras and they are located in the lower abdomen, upper abdomen, heart, neck and upper head. In the Taoist system, we speak of only three main chakras (or dan diens) that lie in the navel, chest and head.

There are dozens of different understandings of the location of the energy channels and the chakras in the various mystical schools around the world and it is not the purpose of this book to describe and compare them all. Interested readers may refer to the book *Circuit of the Force* by Dion Fortune in which she attempts to compare the different energy models of yoga, Tibetan Buddhism and the Kabbalah. For now, it is only important to know that there are many different kundalini energy models in the world and this fact alone should make us a bit sceptical and stop us fixating on just one of them and then make it into a dogma. Instead, we should use these different models as a rough guide and then investigate our mind and body to discover what is really going on. Only then will we be successful at dissolving all our mental and physical blockages - as I will explain in later chapters. In myself and in the work with my clients, I have found that the chakras roughly correspond to the following inner experiences:

Head (in the middle of the brain): thoughts, beliefs, values (positive and negative)
Throat self-confidence, expression of self, sense of fairness (or lack thereof)
Heart (in the middle of the chest): love, compassion, care (or lack thereof)
Solar plexus (below the rib cage): commitment, emotional security, peacefulness (or lack thereof)
Navel (in or just below the belly button): power, courage, assertiveness (or lack thereof)
Root (in the genitals): physical pleasure, physical security (or lack thereof)

Another problem with a rigid model of energy channels is that it invites us to view the kundalini process as something materialistic. You can then easily lose sight of the fact that we are dealing primarily with a mental process in which problems come about through our faulty thoughts and feelings and that we are not dealing with a plumbing system in the body with quasi-physical "blockages" or energy that has accidentally risen in "false channels". Having such a view can easily lead us to pathologise the kundalini process and see ourselves as poor victims who have the misfortune of suffering from energy problems.

As I explained earlier, all energy phenomena are only emotions that have not yet been recognised as such. Many of my clients find this hard to believe because their symptoms truly feel like real streams of energy which painfully jam up, cramp or cause blockages in certain parts of the body. I know such feelings only too well because I have lived with them almost all my life. However, if you learn to recognise all these confusing phenomena as emotions, all the pain and drama often dissolves within a few minutes because emotions usually subside quite quickly. It is the not-recognising of the emotions in our energy symptoms that sometimes keeps them alive for years and can lead to much unnecessary suffering and pain.

Instead of imagining rigid energy channels, one of my Tibetan Buddhist teachers taught us to see the human energy system (which, as I already mentioned, consists exclusively of positive and negative emotions) like a river with many different currents. These currents are not within clearly separated channels but just lie side by side, mix, cross over and generally travel from one place to another just like water currents in a real river. For example, anxiety may be felt in the solar plexus, then moves to the throat and then quickly turns into blissful happiness (as the water turns into steam).

In my experience, everyone has a personal and unique energy (or emotional) system but there are typical patterns and developments. For instance, many people have blockages in their lower chakras, which come from the suppression of their sexual and aggressive impulses. Most people feel fear in their solar plexus, feelings of loneliness in the heart chakra and the infamous head pressure is usually triggered by overly positive beliefs about oneself.

I would also like to question the classical energy model as taught in some yoga schools in which the kundalini rises from the lower chakras, slowly "struggles up" through the blockages in the different chakras until it reaches the top of the head and then automatically leads to enlightenment. I have never seen such an orderly development - neither in any of my clients nor in myself. Rather, it works in such a way that at some point in the kundalini process you experience a first glimpse of an enlightenment state. These glimpses occur more and more often as you progress on your spiritual path. But even advanced practitioners can experience "blocks" in different chakras that need to be worked on before the enlightenment experiences can be stabilised.

In the course of this book, I will explain exactly how to resolve all these blocks. In the next step, one can learn to let the entire energy system be flooded with great bliss. Through the experience of bliss, we can free ourselves from all of our pain-producing attachment to our limited ego and unite completely with the deity. A rigid fixation on certain models of energy channels and chakras will hinder this development rather than promote it and I, therefore, advise against clinging too much to these teachings.

The hourglass personality model

In order to better understand the kundalini process, it is helpful to have a personality model that accommodates this dynamic. The following model is hypothetical but it explains very well how our consciousness changes in a kundalini awakening. According to this concept, our sense of identity looks like an hourglass which is open both at the top and the bottom - as shown in the picture below. It has three parts: the normal ego consciousness, the higher consciousness and the subconscious mind.

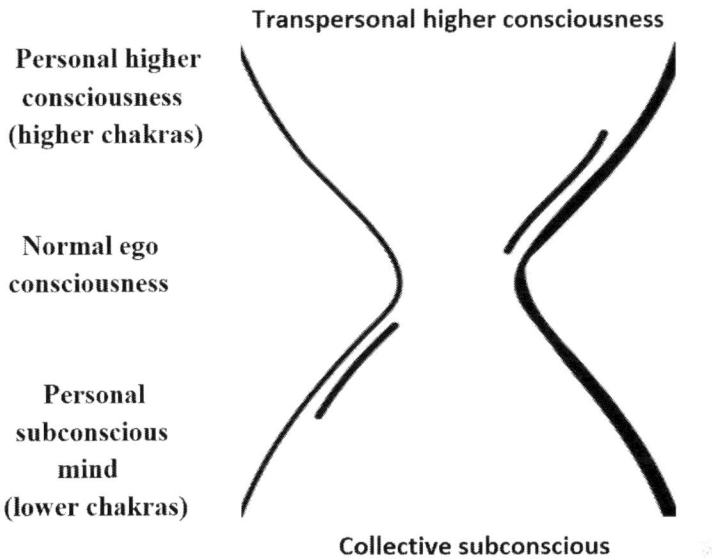

Transpersonal higher consciousness

Personal higher consciousness (higher chakras)

Normal ego consciousness

Personal subconscious mind (lower chakras)

Collective subconscious

The subconscious mind

The subconscious mind is like a warehouse with all our memories that we have largely forgotten but that we can bring back under certain conditions. These memories can be neutral, positive or traumatic in nature. Our subconscious mind also includes all the sensations that we do not need right now, such as background noise or unpleasant odours that are filtered out. Furthermore, in our unconscious mind we find all our unacceptable and anti-social impulses and attitudes, such as aggression, sadism, inappropriate sexual desires, racism, sexism, etc.

As we can see in the picture, the subconscious begins with more personal material and then widens at the bottom of the hourglass into the collective unconscious, which is infinite. Before our kundalini awakening, the lower and upper parts of the hourglass are "frozen", which means we are unconscious of those areas - as I explained in the block of ice metaphor. Through the melting process of the kundalini, we experience an expansion of our consciousness and thus gain more and more access to the material that was previously suppressed. Among other things, this means that all our sense perceptions, emotions and mental impressions appear amplified. Also, we gradually remember all our

21

repressed traumas and we also become more aware of all our anti-social impulses.

Where the hourglass opens into the collective subconscious, we can even have hellish experiences, see demons or have other horror visions that have seemingly nothing to do with our personal history. It is, however, important to understand that we will only have experiences of such a nature when we have a personal affinity to them and therefore have given them some kind of permission to enter into our conscious mind. These things never just happen by accident and I will explain in the seventh chapter how to reduce these kinds of experiences and even switch them off completely.

The subconscious mind in the lower part of the hourglass corresponds in most people with their lower chakras, which are the energy centres in the solar plexus, navel and genitals. Through the kundalini process, we experience more and more feelings (or energy) in these chakras, such as periods of extreme sexual arousal or hunger for power and aggression. But not all feelings in the lower chakras are selfish and aggressive. When the kundalini develops positively, we are gradually able to transform all negative feelings and impulses in the lower chakras into bliss and use their immense power to achieve all our goals easily, most importantly the goal of spiritual enlightenment.

The higher consciousness

The higher consciousness, just like the subconscious mind, begins in the narrower part of the hourglass in a more personal way and expands into the entire universe at the open end at the top of the hourglass and, therefore, ultimately allows us to experience oneness with the divine. Such experiences have been shown to be very similar in different people from different historical times and cultures. For this reason, we call the area above the hourglass "transpersonal", which means going beyond the personal. It is solely through this transpersonal expansion of our mind that it is possible to attain enlightenment. If we could not access the transpersonal higher consciousness, our limitations would always hold us back.

The higher consciousness is situated in most people in the higher chakras, i.e. in the heart, throat and head. These chakras, however, may also be "poisoned" by aggressive or sadistic impulses in undeveloped people. One should, therefore, be careful not to over-simplify the upper chakras as "good" and the lower chakras as "bad". On the contrary, by becoming aware of the repressed and negative parts in our lower chakras during the kundalini process, we get the chance to liberate all chakras (or parts of our minds) and thus become able to use the lower chakras' great power and energy for our spiritual ideals in the upper chakras. Only through this dynamic is the unfolding of our highest potential - or enlightenment - possible. The point is that our *entire* willpower needs to be geared towards wholesome goals in *all* areas of our lives. In this process, a person will experience ever-greater creativity, an ever more accurate intuition and eventually be able to unite completely with a divine being.

Our consciousness always expands simultaneously into the upper and lower parts of the hourglass. Connecting back to the block of ice metaphor, it means that the ice always melts simultaneously in the area of the higher consciousness and of the subconscious mind. Therefore, when we experience beautiful blissful feelings on a meditation retreat, we can expect to experience more unpleasant feelings and memories arising from our subconscious mind over the coming hours or days. Conversely, if you are deeply immersed in the exploration of your subconscious mind within psychotherapy, you will often notice that your capacity for happiness and positive spiritual experiences increases, as well.

It varies from person to person whether the kundalini process (or consciousness expansion) first opens the higher consciousness (the ice melts in the higher chakras) or the subconscious mind (the ice in the lower chakras melts). In traditional textbooks about kundalini, the process is generally described as starting with the root or navel chakra and then rises in an orderly manner chakra by chakra up to the crown. In my therapy practice, however, I have seen this process start with any chakra and open the awareness of the area that the chakra stands for. Moreover, any further development did not necessarily run in an orderly fashion from chakra to chakra but in an idiosyncratic pattern.

The normal ego consciousness

The normal ego consciousness as people experience it before a kundalini awakening corresponds exclusively to the narrow middle part of the hourglass and therefore covers only a very small area of the subconscious mind and the higher consciousness. Such people will often vehemently deny having any anti-social impulses deep inside themselves and they will also question the existence of higher spiritual experiences beyond ordinary religious dogma. For this reason, they are like colour-blind people who accuse people who can see colours (that is, who have spiritual experiences) of having delusions.

Our ego-consciousness works both as an antenna as well as a transmitter and can, therefore, send and receive information to and from the higher consciousness and the subconscious mind as well as to and from other people. For this reason, we can learn to communicate with our higher consciousness through prayer or channelling and also receive answers through intuition and dreams. We can also learn to communicate with our subconscious mind, for example through psychotherapeutic methods, dreams, meditation or by speaking with it directly as we would speak with a small child.

In the kundalini process, the amount of information that we need to process through accessing our higher consciousness, our subconscious mind and also the subconscious minds of others is extremely enlarged and can lead to much confusion and sometimes exhaustion. Also, there are all the intensified sense perceptions that we need to learn to deal with - like light that is too bright, clothing that is too tight and loud noises that are difficult to tolerate. Moreover, we may suddenly have incredibly beautiful spiritual experiences but they are confusing because, simultaneously, we also have frequent periods of intense negative thoughts, feelings and nightmares. On top of that, traumatic memories may suddenly emerge that we find difficult to handle. We also have to learn to deal with paranormal phenomena that can sometimes be frightening and learn how to integrate them constructively into our life. And if all this is not

24

already enough, we also constantly get "information" from other people that they would like to keep secret from us and that we do not always want to know (e.g. when someone finds us sexually attractive or has hidden aggressions towards us). Therefore, it is understandable that in the beginning stages of a kundalini awakening, we may experience much confusion, fear and sometimes despair. But with good guidance, we can learn, bit by bit, how to deal with all these new phenomena and make them a part of our new, expanded sense of self.

When a person is very underdeveloped, their ego-consciousness is identical with the lower (undeveloped) part of the hourglass before the suppression of animalistic and anti-social impulses has taken place. This may be the case, for example, for sadistic psychopaths and to a lesser extent for all other personality disorders. The existence of a subconscious mind is therefore already a first higher development and ideally should have taken place during our childhood through the education process. A second higher development happens through the kundalini awakening and makes the subconscious mind conscious again and thereby enables us to use the energy that was trapped inside it to grow on the spiritual path. This path is called the tantric or kundalini path or the Vajrayana path in Tibetan Buddhism. This path is only suitable for people who have learnt to reliably suppress all their animalistic, aggressive and anti-social impulses and can resist the temptation to act on these impulses once they resurface during a kundalini awakening. If this is not the case, a kundalini awakening will be abused for egoistic purposes and produce charismatic individuals who may act as charlatans or cult leaders to exploit and abuse gullible and naïve people.

Integration of the subconscious mind with the higher consciousness
A person with expanded consciousness always has access to the narrow part of the hourglass that is considered to be normal in our society and they can also communicate with people who only have limited access to their higher consciousness and their subconscious mind. But many of my clients fear that there is something wrong with them because they cannot communicate the experiences from their higher consciousness or their

subconscious mind without disapproval, fearful reactions or even a diagnosis of mental illness. It is therefore of great importance to strengthen the self-confidence of people in the kundalini process so that they know that there is nothing wrong with them but, quite the contrary, very much right. They are, as it were, like highly gifted children who cannot cope in a normal school because they lack the right support.

Some people with awakened kundalini may object at this point and say that they do not feel gifted at all but feel rather overwhelmed by the kundalini process. The answer is that feeling overwhelmed results from a mixture of misinformation, a lack of guidance and too much material emerging too quickly from their subconscious mind. Once these people get help dealing with the opening of their subconscious mind, they are also quickly able to enjoy the delights of the higher consciousness.

The healing modality of higher-consciousness healing that I'll explain in the fourth chapter supports people in this process. It connects them more strongly to the upper part of the hourglass by focusing on their higher power in their hearts. This healing practice will also help them to deal with the sometimes very embarrassing or painful material emerging from their subconscious mind by focusing on compassionate love for themselves and others. The visualisation of a bubble around them will help them to have strong and clear boundaries so that they can handle all the new information and perceptions that are constantly coming in through their expanded consciousness.

The aim of a kundalini awakening is to gain access to our entire higher consciousness and our entire subconscious mind, transform and heal all pain-inflicting beliefs and feelings and finally integrate the upper and lower parts of the hourglass harmoniously. However, as both parts of our consciousness are ultimately infinitely large, this process will continue indefinitely. This shows that the idea of static and complete enlightenment is incorrect. Instead, we should prepare to embark on a lifelong process of an ever-expanding awareness through which we receive ever more information that we can use for the benefit of all beings. The Swedish mystic Emanuel Swedenborg expressed this fact by saying that each person carries the whole of heaven and the whole hell within themselves and that it was our task to choose heaven from moment to moment.

The kundalini process will unfold most harmoniously if we can create a balance between the upper and lower parts of the hourglass - or the higher and lower chakras - within us. Many people make the mistake of concentrating too much on either the upper or the lower chakras and thus create an imbalance in themselves. For example, most traditional religions focus solely on the "good" in the higher chakras (wisdom and love) and demonise the "lower instincts" of the lower chakras (power, aggression and sexuality). Many mystical or esoteric schools also focus too much on beautiful experiences of light and love and do not provide enough support in dealing with the simultaneously emerging material from the subconscious mind. As a result, many religious and spiritual people suffer from unnecessary guilt, confusion, and psychosomatic problems due to their inability to deal with their shadow side, which increasingly pushes itself into their consciousness.

On the other hand, many forms of psychotherapy are "digging" too much into the subconscious mind (in the lower chakras) to bring suppressed feelings and memories to light. In this process, they neglect the liberating and healing power of the higher consciousness. As a result, many psychotherapy clients get stuck in strong negative feelings without a chance to truly heal themselves.

A harmonious integration of the liberated higher and lower chakras means that we have more and more beautiful spiritual experiences of oneness while willingly accept a life-long purification process of our subconscious mind. In this way, we can hope for complete healing of our past and the positive development of our highest spiritual potential in the future. On the other hand, if we develop too much power without love, we will become selfish tyrants and if we develop too much love without power then we become a bit useless. Only by combining our power and our loving wisdom can we realise our highest potential of "loving power" or "powerful love" and thus help other people as well.

It is therefore a fact that only through the kundalini process or the tantric spiritual path do we have the unique opportunity to transform the raw power of the lower chakras and thereby strengthen the love and wisdom of the higher chakras. For this reason, we should feel highly privileged that we now have the good fortune of this extraordinary expansion of consciousness and joyfully go to work to overcome all the challenges on this path.

The Kundalini process is changing us for the better

I have already explained in the hourglass personality model that a kundalini awakening is essentially an extension of our consciousness. Therefore, we experience everything that goes on in our minds more intensively and this process also brings unconscious material into our awareness. This applies to content coming from our subconscious mind as well as to content coming from our higher consciousness. For this reason, a kundalini awakening equally offers us the opportunity to reach enlightenment and the opportunity to become extraordinary evil.

It is much easier to choose to pursue our good and healthy potential when we can acknowledge that we are split into two fundamentally different sides than if we completely deny that we have any immoral impulses. It is exactly because of such a denial that we fall prey much more easily to our unconscious anti-social impulses while self-righteously insisting that we are "good people".

A person in the kundalini process becomes increasingly aware of their dark aspects, for example, tendencies towards racism, sexism and all other forms of discrimination against minorities and weaker people. They also recognise, for example, how much petty envy, greed and animalistic aggression is working in their mind. At the same time, they also have more interior space to simply let these impulses pass by and do not compulsively act them out as people with less awareness often do. So, paradoxically, it is the realisation of our potential for evil that protects us from actually becoming evil. It works that way because we can only control things that we are aware of. People in the kundalini process seldom adamantly claim to be "good people" but rather say something like, "I always try to do the good and the right thing but, unfortunately, I do not always succeed."

Some of my clients develop excessive feelings of guilt due to this dynamic and need a little help to see that they are not "bad people" just because they suddenly find aggressive or envious impulses in themselves that they did not see before. I will describe later how to let go of this excessive guilt.

In most people, the awakening of the kundalini strengthens their motivation to make every area of their life better, healthier and more spiritual. This may begin with a desire to use gentler medicine in healthcare and a desire to resolve psychosomatic problems through psychotherapy rather than suppressing them with drugs. People typically develop a strong desire to eat healthier foods and often become vegetarians or vegans. In relationships, they wish for more honesty, authenticity and love. Consequently, there can be drastic - but positive - changes in how they relate to their family of origin, in their relationships with their partner, their children and friends. People will only stay in close friendship with those who also wish to move to a higher level of consciousness. To all the others, they will create more distance and sometimes relationships have to end altogether. This often happens when people have allowed themselves to be exploited or even abused by others. As the kundalini awakening progresses, such "tolerance" will become impossible because the suffering becomes too intense. In that sense, the kundalini process "forces" us to abandon unhealthy relationships and replace them with healthier ones. People are most likely to find new friendships in spiritual groups where they often find new "families", too. The process of transforming our relationships can never be easy or quick and I will discuss this topic in detail in the eighth chapter.

At work, there are often many changes as well and I see in virtually all of my kundalini clients that they prefer to work in a helping profession and are sometimes even willing to make a complete career change if they feel their current work has not enough spiritual value. Many people also perceive their working environment as increasingly unbearable if they are not lucky enough to be surrounded by especially kind and spiritually conscious work colleagues. For this reason, they often seek self-employment.

29

Some people worry that they might lose their talents and positive traits when they are experiencing many negative kundalini symptoms. Fortunately, this is not the case. On the contrary, since the kundalini acts as a form of amplifier of ourselves, our talents and positive traits will also be enhanced in this process. Ultimately, the kundalini power will allow us to become more successful in everything we do.

Many people in the kundalini process seek solitude and silence - both at home and on vacation - and usually loathe large gatherings where people enjoy themselves in traditional ways such as a carnival or a huge tourist hotel. All rough, loud and selfish behaviour becomes increasingly repugnant and this great sensitivity sometimes causes a lot of pain and confusion because people feel less and less at home in the so-called "normal society". Here it can help to know that you are not alone with these feelings and you are certainly not crazy. On the contrary, this is a higher development that can only unfold well when it is recognised as such. Stronger sensitivity can be compared to a form of higher intelligence. Through the perception of subtle impulses that remain invisible to ordinary people, we can look deep into the unconscious minds of ourselves and others and also experience the ecstatic nature of our minds and, ultimately, the very essence of ourselves and the entire universe.

It will not always be easy to explain these realms to people who have no access to them, just as a maths professor would find it difficult to explain to non-mathematicians what she is working on. But despite these comprehension problems, we ourselves, as well as therapists and physicians, should never forget that the heightened sensitivity in the kundalini process is a higher development and certainly not a disease.

If we apply ourselves to our spiritual disciplines, the kundalini process can with time bring many gifts and graces - the so-called supernatural powers (or siddhis) and ultimately enlightenment. Since this book is more about overcoming painful kundalini symptoms, I will only briefly touch upon these supernatural gifts. They are described in more detail in my first kundalini book *Enlightenment through the Path of Kundalini*. These abilities include increased creativity, clairvoyance, telepathy, spiritual healing, and many others. Every human being has these gifts as seeds already within themselves but it needs the intensified awareness of a kundalini awakening to make them accessible and much spiritual practice to really make them blossom. For this reason, it is important to understand that a first kundalini awakening is just a gate through which we must go in order to develop over the course of many years the many gifts that this process allows us to access.

Another gift that can evolve through a kundalini awakening is the ability to manifest our desires. People have this ability to a certain extent even before a kundalini awakening and many books describe this process, which is often referred to as "the law of attraction". What these books do not mention, however, is the fact that manifestation power only flourishes properly through the awakening of the kundalini. I myself have consciously manifested virtually every aspect of my life in this way and my own story is, therefore, evidence that these abilities actually exist. If you want to know more about this topic, I recommend my book *Advanced Manifesting*, which explains in detail how to do this in practice.

As desirable and beautiful supernatural abilities are, they also represent the greatest danger in the kundalini process because you can get lost in them and, unfortunately, also corrupted. If you have achieved a certain degree of clairvoyance, for example, and offer readings for money, there is the danger that you will start to lie when you have a bad day and do not have good access to your intuition. Another gift that is often abused is the power to fascinate (also called charisma). I think most people have heard of spiritual teachers who have abused their power to fascinate for their own selfish desires.

Most of my clients have strong ethical principles and do not need such warnings. Unfortunately, I sometimes had to witness such abuse of kundalini powers - both among my clients and my colleagues. An American therapist who offers kundalini support - as several clients told me - demanded, for example, that they should undress during their therapy sessions. I have also heard that he tried to have sex with many of his clients - supposedly to help them. Of course, all of this is a terrible abuse of his position and I tell this story to warn my readers not to be gullible and trust everyone. Unfortunately, a kundalini awakening does not guarantee ethical correctness.

Luckily, the kundalini process has a profound humbling influence on most people. This humility is also referred to in spiritual literature as ego-dissolution and we usually experience this process as painful and unpleasant. Nobody likes to be forced to be humble because we all have open or hidden desires to be admired or even be adored. But the expansion of consciousness in the kundalini process quickly exposes such egotistical desires as completely ridiculous because we can no longer indulge in our self-aggrandising illusions as unconsciously as before. However, despite the "whining" of our ego, humility is wonderfully liberating because we can finally really be ourselves without constantly having to wear a mask. This new authenticity allows us to enter into deeper relationships with other people and with the Divine and experience such great blessings that make the unpleasant ego dissolution process worthwhile.

The greatest transformation in the kundalini process is our ability to experience a deeply felt spirituality. We will find incredible joy, comfort, and meaning in all aspects of our religious and spiritual lives so that our worldly goals and pleasures become less and less important. Most of my clients find this spirituality in unorthodox groups but some of my clients successfully live their new spirituality in the context of traditional religions.

The greatest gift in the kundalini process is the ability to experience and stabilise higher spiritual states and insights. These can be intense states of spiritual ecstasy, deep insights into the nature of reality, the ability to love deeply and even experiences of union with the Divine, which can also be called enlightenment. Even before a kundalini awakening, it is possible to experience such states of mind for brief moments but only the energy of the kundalini will make it possible to stabilise them. However, it is important to understand that the stabilisation of higher spiritual states of mind will not be automatic and will only happen if people channel their kundalini awakening into a regular and intensive spiritual practice. In contrast, people who are against spiritual practice and fight the expansion of their consciousness will experience this process as a form of great suffering.

What is enlightenment?

The real purpose of a kundalini awakening is not attaining all the supernatural abilities, the ability for wish fulfilments or frequent states of bliss but it is complete enlightenment. To better understand this term, it is important to know that in Buddhism the highest spiritual development is called "awakening" and not "enlightenment". The term "awakening" indicates that this is a kind of higher dimension that will be recognised immediately as "the real reality", where we are more "ourselves", just as when we awaken from a nightmare and recognise that it was "only a dream" and that we are now back to our "real life".

In Tibetan Buddhism, there is a metaphor of a house that beautifully explains the spiritual path and enlightenment. In this image, the foundation of the house represents ethical behaviour, the walls of the house are made of love and compassion and the roof consists of the bliss of the realisation of our true, divine nature. Without the foundation of moral behaviour, all our efforts on our spiritual path are on unstable ground and the walls of our house of enlightenment will sooner or later collapse. Likewise, all the experiences of blissful unity with the divine are useless unless the walls of love and compassion are firmly established in our mind. Without them, the roof would fall to the ground and shatter - just as all our beautiful spiritual experiences will be quickly destroyed by constant quarrels in hostile relationships.

Even if we succeed in building the whole house with a foundation of moral behaviour, walls of love and a roof of spiritual bliss, it will still be meaningless if we are not ready to use the house for its intended purpose. The true meaning of the house is to be a shelter for suffering beings so that they can seek refuge and receive spiritual teachings and build their own houses. In other words, enlightenment means being a truly loving person who has recognised their divine nature. If you want to learn more about this highest spiritual state, please refer to my books *Enlightenment through the Path of Kundalini, Spiritual Joy* and *Stairway to Heaven.*

Kundalini is mainly a process of the mind

I have had many clients who feared that the kundalini had caused them physical harm. Some clients suspected, for example, that the kundalini had burnt their nerves, harmed their body tissue or destroyed their inner organs. Some clients also suspected that their brains were somehow injured, that their skin was damaged or that their fatigue was a sign that their health had taken a turn for the worse. I also saw several cases where my clients were convinced that they would soon die.

Many of my clients had already been to several doctors before they came to me and I always send all other clients who have physical symptoms to a doctor to rule any actual diseases. In all the years of my work, it only happened twice that a client came back from a doctor with an actual diagnosis. In neither case was the illness related to the painful symptoms that had brought them to me. All other clients told me that the doctor had not found anything wrong with them. Once we had this green light, I could begin to dissolve all the physical pain, negative feelings and fatigue purely through psychotherapy. My success rate with this approach I would estimate as over 90%.

In principle, this approach works like this: I ask my clients to imagine that what appears to be their physical symptom is actually an emotion and that the emotion can say something. In most cases, once the message of the emotion is revealed, it takes us around 5 to 10 minutes for the physical pain or fatigue to begin to subside. If the client continues to practise diligently at home, these symptoms usually disappear within a few days or weeks.

Unfortunately, there are books and websites which spread the idea that the kundalini is fundamentally a biological process and can cause much physical damage. Through my consistent positive results derived purely from psychotherapy, I consider these opinions to be wrong and misleading. If the body could really be damaged in the kundalini process then physicians would surely find something wrong with my clients every now and then. It would also be impossible to get rid of painful symptoms with simple visualisation exercises within minutes. These fast healing results are an indication that the problem is located in the energy or

34

emotional body and can be best treated at this level.

In my opinion, it is the *fear* of physical injury that aggravates all the symptoms and prevents the true solution. If we are prepared to treat our symptoms as coming from our mind (of course only when we have received the go-ahead from the medical profession), very simple techniques are often enough to make all the pain disappear quickly. I will show in the sixth chapter how to proceed in detail. For the moment, I want to provide further evidence that the whole kundalini process is a spiritual and energetic development, not a physical one.

As I explained in the block of ice metaphor, the rising of the kundalini allows many suppressed emotions to emerge from our unconscious mind and it is scientifically proven that emotions affect our body. Anger and bitterness, for example, negatively affect our immune system while feelings of joy and love strengthen it. When we are anxious, we often tense up physically and our hearts may start to race. When we feel love, we relax again. The kundalini in itself is not the same as these feelings but it is the expanded consciousness that makes our previously suppressed emotions visible. The kundalini is, therefore, to be seen as neutral in this process - much like money that can be spent for wholesome or unwholesome purposes. It is up to us to cultivate positive emotions in our mind or indulge for an unnecessarily long time in negative ones - producing either positive or negative effects in our physical body. It is not the kundalini directly that is doing this.

A woman once told me that she had paralysis in her foot and that she was able to convince her neurologist that the kundalini had done this damage to her body. However, symptoms of paralysis in the limbs without a physical cause are classic conversion symptoms that have nothing at all to do with the kundalini process. Conversion symptoms result from suppressed emotions and cause symptoms such as paralysis, blindness or fainting. These symptoms were formerly called hysteria until this term was abolished as being too discriminatory.

The conversion syndrome is similar to physical kundalini symptoms, such as pain, with the difference that it is much more persistent. This means that it is much more difficult to make the cause of the symptoms conscious compared to physical kundalini symptoms. More importantly, conversion symptoms lead to real functional impairments of the body, which is not part of the kundalini syndrome. Conversion syndrome can occur in people with or without kundalini. So, there are people with awakened kundalini who also suffer from conversion symptoms. I had a small number of such clients and I have also achieved positive results in these cases by proceeding in the same way as I do with pure kundalini symptoms. However, the therapeutic process usually took longer.

To properly understand the kundalini process, we should imagine that our physical body is permeated and brought alive by an energetic body and a mental body. The energetic body consists entirely of emotions while the mental body is made up of thoughts. When a person dies, the physical body separates from these two other bodies and becomes lifeless.

Before a kundalini awakening, most people are reasonably aware of their physical body because they can see it. But they often perceive their energetic and mental bodies only sporadically. Because of this they may, for instance, act in a passive-aggressive way because they cannot acknowledge their anger and they may suppress many negative emotions because they are trying to be "cool" or "nice". We can imagine that the kundalini process dramatically increases our perception of all three bodies so that it becomes impossible to go through life as unconsciously as before.

Despite their increased awareness, many people in the kundalini process still only perceive their feelings in a semi-conscious way. These emotions are kind of "stuck" halfway between the subconscious mind and the conscious mind and are perceived as the typical physical "energy" symptoms such as trembling, twitching, pain and pressure in many different body parts. Many of my clients are surprised when I tell them that these symptoms are all emotions of which they are only half-aware. But when I help them to "translate" their physical symptoms into emotions and dissolve them, they can see that my theory is correct.

Many of my clients also find my statement that our energy body consists entirely of thoughts and emotions very strange because they believe that all sorts of other "energies" haunt them and cause problems. They therefore often use expressions such as, "the kundalini is unbearable today" or "the kundalini is giving me a lot of pain". These expressions are incorrect because the kundalini in itself does nothing except expand our perception. What is "strong" and perhaps hurts are our feelings, which are more or less unconscious and therefore cannot be released.

To achieve healing, it is therefore of the highest importance to deepen our perception in order to recognise the emotions in all of our strange and frightening physical symptoms together with the erroneous beliefs that keep them going. Once these thoughts and emotions have been recognised, they can be quickly resolved with higher-consciousness healing. The following case study describes what this looks like in practice. Later in this book, I will describe in detail how anyone can follow this process themselves.

Case study:

Harry was a successful singer and had been suffering from many kundalini symptoms when he contacted me. He cried for hours every day, was extremely exhausted and felt overwhelmed with many situations in his life that he could master well before. I showed him the higher-consciousness healing and we applied it to the sorrow that he felt, which was like being an unloved child. The core of the higher-consciousness healing was to connect to his own higher consciousness and receive love and protection from this divine mother or father. This meditation quickly gave Harry much comfort and reassurance and alleviated his sadness. I also showed him how he could easily switch off his prolonged crying spells by sitting up and keeping his whole spine very straight.

In the next phase of therapy, we explored why he felt so stressed and exhausted all the time and worked out that he tried to get all his social contacts through a complicated network of friends but that this never really satisfied him. On the contrary, the many contacts with his friends stressed him because he constantly ran from one appointment to another to keep his feelings of loneliness at bay.

Harry's worst symptom was a burning pain in the skin of his upper body. I asked Harry to feel into this pain and ask himself which emotion was most similar to this pain - fear, anger or sadness. After a brief examination, he said, "grief". I asked Harry to imagine that there was a mouth in the centre of the pain and asked him to find words to express this grief. When Harry started to speak, his tears began to flow again and he spoke of his fear of entering into a deep love relationship with a woman.

I encouraged Harry to mentally imagine a wonderful relationship that was exactly how he wanted it to be. It only took a few minutes for the burning pain in Harry's body to diminish significantly, which was very unusual for him. Within a few weeks of repeating this practice, his pain completely disappeared and at the same time his fears, sadness and exhaustion improved or completely vanished.

After another few months, Harry began a love relationship with a woman that was much more genuine, authentic and fulfilling than anything he had experienced before. Now and then, his symptoms flared up again but he could always handle them quickly by using higher-consciousness healing.

The kundalini test

I have already mentioned that there is very little literature or scientific studies about the phenomenon of kundalini, so I see myself as a kind of pioneer in this field. The author who, in my opinion, deals with the topic most thoroughly and rationally is Yvonne Kason in her book *Farther Shores.* Other notable authors are Bonnie Greenwell and Lee Sanella.

To my knowledge, no recognised test can be used to diagnose a kundalini awakening and I, therefore, developed a simple and reliable test myself based on my experience with over a thousand clients. In order to use this test, you should think of the time when you suspect that you had your kundalini awakening. This time can be a short, powerful experience or it can be a phase extending a few weeks or months. Then you look at all the years before and the time after this turning point. The test suggests you had a kundalini awakening if you notice the following five changes:

Increased interest in spirituality and religiosity and the desire to make your life healthier, more loving and more meaningful in every way. This desire might manifest in reading more spiritual books, meditating and praying, and making spirituality and personal development the centre of your life. There are cases in which people have an initial increased interest in spirituality but then become so scared that they stop meditating and even try to turn away from spirituality. You would still score a "yes" in such a case. You would also score a "yes" if you were strongly interested in spirituality before your awakening and your interest remained the same after the awakening. High or increased interest in spirituality is the most important point in this test. Without it, the other four points on this list do not constitute a kundalini awakening.

Increased sensitivity: Light may appear as too bright, the sun too hot, noises too loud and odours as disgusting. On the other hand, music or the natural world may feel overwhelmingly beautiful. You may also be more sensitive to atmospheres and "vibrations" or "energy", which can be either positive or negative experiences.

Intensified emotions: You experience positive and negative emotions in an intensity that you never have experienced before. Many of my clients suffer from high anxiety, sadness, despair or anger. But sooner or later, the pendulum also swings in the other direction and people experience ecstasies or hours of orgasmic bliss that are generally unknown to people without kundalini.

Experiences of energy movements in the body: You feel energy moving in your body, such as rising heat, snake-like movements, pressure feelings, tremors, strange pains and much more.

Paranormal experiences: These are experiences such as extremely unlikely "coincidences", clairvoyance, telepathy, encounters with the dead, visions, experiences with spirits and divine beings. Some people also suddenly realise that they can heal others by the laying on of hands. In some people, this fifth point is missing. If all other four elements are strong, I would regard it as a mild kundalini awakening in its beginning stages.

Differential diagnosis of kundalini syndrome

The five criteria above describe the general symptoms of a kundalini awakening. The more mature and conscious a person was before their awakening, the more the positive aspects of this process will predominate and bring spiritual insights, bliss and, ultimately, supernatural abilities. This would be the perfect scenario but I would think that it is very rare even though I cannot prove this statement as such people rarely come to my practice.

When the painful, frightening and confusing symptoms predominate we speak of the so-called kundalini syndrome. One should bear in mind, however, that kundalini syndrome is not a mental illness or neurosis but is still fundamentally an expansion of consciousness, which is always a higher development even if it is very challenging at times. It is mainly the lack of information that can lead people to confuse it with various mental disorders and thus create even more fear than necessary.

Kundalini syndrome can be confused with the following diseases and disorders: drug psychosis, burn-out, conversion syndrome, bipolar disorder, post-traumatic stress disorder, various personality disorders and psychotic illness. The most important difference between these mental problems and kundalini syndrome is the active desire for spirituality and health, which are central for someone with a kundalini awakening but tends to decrease with the other disorders.

Unfortunately, mental issues can occur simultaneously with kundalini syndrome and for this reason, it can be difficult to draw a clear line between these states. However, I would like reassure my readers already now that, in my opinion, a psychosis through a kundalini awakening only happens very rarely and only if a person has a disposition for such an illness.

In the following paragraphs, I will highlight the main distinguishing features between kundalini syndrome and other psychological disorders.

Drug psychosis: A drug psychosis may happen after ingesting psychotropic substances, such as LSD, magic mushrooms or cannabis, whereby it is irrelevant how much and how often these drugs have been taken. I also had some clients who developed symptoms of drug psychosis after taking shamanic substances like ayahuasca, which are quite fashionable at the moment and are not supposed to trigger psychosis. Unfortunately, I cannot confirm this to be true.

During a drug psychosis, people can experience symptoms similar to a kundalini awakening such as intensified sensitivity, increased emotion (usually fear) and paranormal experiences (usually paranoia and strong confusion). Less likely are energy movements in the body.

Thankfully, a drug psychosis usually resolves all by itself but it may take many months. I have had quite a number of clients who had a kundalini awakening and a drug psychosis simultaneously. The treatment is the same as for the pure kundalini syndrome but one should expect a longer duration of treatment. It is also more difficult to experience positive results with higher-consciousness healing because we are dealing with chemicals in the body and not only with one's mind.

Burn-out: Burn-out is a fashionable term, which is actually a form of depression caused by exhaustion. It is quite possible that a kundalini awakening will be misdiagnosed as burn-out especially when it occurs in people with successful careers who no longer see meaning in their work. Both burn-out and kundalini syndrome can cause severe tiredness and exhaustion, which may make it impossible to continue working. Furthermore, a kundalini awakening and burn-out have in common that people have the desire to re-evaluate their lives and often feel drawn to make major changes.

To distinguish the two states, it is helpful to recognise that only a small number of people with a kundalini awakening suffer from exhaustion and that the strong urge for spirituality is not part of a pure burn-out. Furthermore, during a burn-out, we do not find internal energy movements or paranormal experiences.

Burn-out and a kundalini awakening can occur simultaneously. With higher-consciousness healing, we can resolve fatigue and tiredness quite quickly, as I will explain later in the book. A career change can also be helpful to direct one's life in a more meaningful and spiritual direction.

41

Conversion syndrome: As explained earlier, conversion syndrome is caused by suppressed emotion and may manifest in paralysis, blindness or fainting spells. Such disturbances were described by the founder of psychoanalysis - Sigmund Freud - and we can assume that a sexually repressive culture contributes to such problems. But conversion symptoms still occur today and I have had several clients with this problem. It differs from kundalini syndrome by causing actual physical dysfunction, which means that the patients are actually paralysed or blind and not just imagining or faking it. By contrast, physical kundalini symptoms are limited to pain, inner heat, tiredness, involuntary movements (kriyas), tremors and twitching. Also, conversion syndrome does not necessarily lead to a feeling of inner energy movements, intensified emotions or increased sensitivity. Conversion patients can sometimes appear highly emotional (literally "hysterical") but these emotions are often not genuine but are overdramatisations that are used to (unconsciously) manipulate other people. Unfortunately, it is often difficult to differentiate between these two types of intensified emotions.

If you suspect that you have conversion syndrome, you should seek medical advice to exclude all physical causes. After that clarification has been done, you can continue with purely psychotherapeutic work. Unfortunately, in the treatment of conversion syndrome, it is much more difficult to get to the unconscious feelings of the client compared to the work with kundalini syndrome. You cannot just ask, "What kind of emotion does your physical pain resemble?" as I do with my kundalini clients.

I have had the best results with conversion clients when they have been consistently willing to treat their symptoms as psychological and radically ignore the physical component. I tell them to say to their body that, "I am no longer interested in all this fuss but only in my emotions". In many cases, the conversion symptoms subsided and the emerging feelings were quickly resolved with higher-consciousness healing. The biggest challenge in this approach is to convince a client that their physical symptoms are only psychological and to stop seeking a physical solution. A good book that describes this approach is *The Mindbody Prescription* by Dr John Sarno.

Bipolar disorder (manic-depressive disorder): This disorder is a mental illness in which phases of mania or elation and depression alternate. To warrant such a diagnosis, there must be a serious impairment of functioning in a person's life - intense feelings of bliss and sadness alone are not a basis for a diagnosis. In a real mania, those affected sometimes accrue high debts through reckless financial decisions and excessive shopping, put themselves at risk through dangerous sexual actions, behave inappropriately in public and may even lose their job or life partner through their irresponsible behaviours.

It is possible to confuse the mania of bipolar disorder with the euphoria and bliss that becomes more intense during the kundalini process. On closer examination, however, it quickly becomes clear that these two states of mind are very different. The mania in bipolar disorder is basically a feeling of restless drivenness in which a person often feels quite irritable and which often leads to irresponsible actions like unrestrained shopping or other risky behaviours. The high spirits in the kundalini process, however, are a form of real bliss, completely free of any form of striving. They are sustained orgasmic feelings in every part of the body accompanied by a feeling of being united with the divine and these states often produce profound spiritual insights. Moreover, these experiences continue to inspire the person even when the joy has subsided whereas, after a mania, people usually feel profound regret and depression.

Sometimes people with bipolar disorder can also experience elated moods but the difference from a kundalini awakening is the fact that people going through the latter always know how to behave like a "normal person". They would not do the inappropriate things a manic person may do such as undressing in public or embarking on a mad shopping frenzy, which they would regret at a later stage.

I had several clients who had a bipolar diagnosis and experienced a kundalini awakening at the same time. Here is the best course of action to strengthen people's insight into their illness: learn to notice the early warning signs (for example, the decreased need for sleep and food) and surround yourself with people who can help before you completely lose control. Depending on the severity of the condition, medication can

43

sometimes be unavoidable.

Borderline, histrionic and narcissitic personality disorders: Borderline and histrionic disorders can lead to very intense emotions just like during a kundalini awakening so that it is possible to confuse both states. The difference is that a person with kundalini syndrome does not impulsively act out their strong emotions and generally tends not to create the over-the-top drama that people with a borderline or histrionic personality disorder do. Nor do we find in people with kundalini syndrome symptoms such as self-harm, self-endangering (sexual) behaviour, addictive beha-viour and the extreme selfishness that are inherent in all personality disorders.

However, it is possible that a kundalini rising brings an already existing mild personality disorder more to the fore due to the general amplification of all mental processes during an awakening. On the one hand, this can cause an exacerbation of the personality disorder symptoms but on the other hand, it also provides a chance to overcome these problems since a person in the kundalini process usually has a strong desire to improve themselves. This also applies to personality disorders which are usually considered to be therapy-resistant. In my experience, the appropriate approach for these people is cognitive therapy (which means changing false beliefs) because their egoism and their desire to dominate others are kept alive by a web of irrational thoughts and beliefs. Unfortunately, working with clients who have personality disorders will always be tough and slow and I see little reason to believe that these problems can be easily overcome.

The narcissistic personality disorder is a special case and can have especially serious consequences because the kundalini awakening also enhances charisma and therefore empowers the unscrupulous narcissist to seduce, manipulate and exploit other people even more skilfully. When such a person has a kundalini awakening, it stimulates in them the desire for more spirituality - just like for all others in this process. Unfortunately, their megalomania will motivate them to announce themselves very quickly as a spiritual teacher who is now entitled to teach and lead others. Through their enhanced charisma, a narcissist with awakened kundalini can often attract gullible and naive people who they can easily exploit. It is precisely this process that is responsible for all the charlatanry and exploitation of spiritual disciples by corrupt "gurus". Those familiar with the "spiritual scene" will know how many of these unfortunate situations exist. This section should therefore also be understood as a warning to always thoroughly examine a potential spiritual teacher before engaging with them.

In a more positive development, a person with a personality disorder may seek a spiritual teacher or therapist and allow that person to "educate" them in order to free themselves from their selfishness and megalomania. This process will never be easy because the ego of these people will always react very angrily towards all criticism. However, through the consciousness expansion in the kundalini process, the personality disordered person may also develop an inkling that their egoism is wrong and for that reason, they may continue their spiritual endeavours, which is, of course, very positive. But I still would like to warn against expecting quick "conversion experiences" with personality disorders because in my experience they are extremely rare.

Post-traumatic stress disorder: This disorder happens after traumatic events that people find hard to let go of. It should be mentioned that some people find the arousal of kundalini in itself traumatic and therefore the symptoms of post-traumatic stress disorder and kundalini syndrome can merge to a certain degree in some people. Symptoms that can occur in both states include distressing emotions, high anxiety, horrific visions and a general feeling of finding it hard to cope.

The differential diagnosis is again that every person with a kundalini awakening develops an intense spiritual interest, which may be completely missing in ordinary post-traumatic stress disorder. Luckily, both problems can be treated in exactly the same way with higher-consciousness healing, which is why it is not so important to tell these two problems exactly apart.

Psychotic disease: Many of my clients are afraid of "becoming crazy" when they come to me but so far not one client has developed a psychosis while they were in therapy with me. I had only one client in whom I suspected psychotic tendencies. This client had tuberculosis and took a drug that could have psychosis as a side effect. So, I'm not necessarily convinced that her confused state of mind was created by the kundalini process.

Another client had been a member of a satanic sect where they experimented with the awakening of "dark energy". She told me that in this process there were regular occurrences of people becoming psychotic and that many members of this sect had ended up in psychiatry. Unfortunately, she was also one of those people. Therefore, I see her crisis mostly as a reaction to the black magic and devil worship that was practised in this sect rather than the result of her kundalini awakening. I also assume that this woman had a certain predisposition to serious mental disorders.

An important distinction between a true psychotic disorder and unwanted and frightening paranormal experiences in the kundalini process is the ability and also the desire to talk about these experiences in detail. People with real mental illnesses usually do not want to talk, while people in the kundalini process typically have a strong desire to share their experiences and often suffer when they have no one who understands them.

Furthermore, people in the kundalini process can often date exactly when their paranormal experiences started and they can also remember how they felt before their kundalini awakening. Psychotic people, on the other hand, lose their ability to distinguish between "normal" and "crazy" thoughts and behaviours. They often behave inappropriately in public and they cannot remember what it is like to be normal.

People in the kundalini process also know at any time that their "weird" experiences are considered as abnormal by general society and can usually judge well how to behave in order not to be declared crazy. It is precisely this awareness about what is normal for normal people that is the indicator of mental health and, as long as it exists in a person, I consider a diagnosis of psychosis as counter-indicated.

As I mentioned earlier, in a kundalini process a person is gaining a new "paranormal" dimension of their mind in addition to their old "normal" dimension, they can distinguish between the two and they are also able to communicate about it all relatively clearly. In contrast, a psychotic client loses the normal dimension of their mind and thinks and behaves in a way that would be considered "crazy" by normal society without being aware of this fact. They would, therefore, reject any feedback that their thoughts and behaviours are inappropriate. By comparison, people in the kundalini process often seek help to understand or eliminate their paranormal experiences because they still have a clear idea of what a normal state of mind consists of.

For these reasons, the term "kundalini psychosis" is completely out of place and I wish it had never been invented. It just creates unnecessary fear and, as I have already mentioned, I have not seen a single kundalini client slide into psychosis except in the rare exception that I described above. However, I have had a number of clients who received a diagnosis of psychosis although they were never psychotic in my opinion. We have to ascribe this troublesome situation to the fact that most physicians and psychiatrists simply look at all frightening paranormal experiences through the lens of their diagnostic catalogue and simply do not know about the phenomenon of a kundalini awakening.

All this is very unfortunate especially when you consider that the problem of "spiritual crisis" was added to the list of psychiatric disorders roughly 20 years ago. When I listen to my clients, it seems to me, however, that most psychiatrists either have not read this section of their diagnostic manual or they do not take it seriously. Many psychiatrists and therapists are atheists and have a strong tendency to dismiss spiritual experiences as old-fashioned superstitions or even as forms of psychosis. They may, therefore, also be very reluctant to engage seriously in conversations about problems with God and paranormal experiences. The "solution" is then a diagnosis of mental illness which is treated with neuroleptics - drugs intended for psychotic and schizophrenic people.

Before we begin to condemn all psychiatrists too much, I would like to say that most clients who have come to me through the psychiatric route had wanted to take this route themselves. Nobody forced them to go into psychiatry and take medication - they usually did this voluntarily because they hoped to be cured through medication. Fortunately, only a very small percentage of my clients took this path.

Through higher-consciousness healing, everyone can learn to deal with the paranormal experiences that can occur on the kundalini path in a positive and empowering way and limit and eradicate unpleasant experiences. It takes a bit of practice and perseverance but, on the whole, my clients always learnt to use these experiences for their own benefit (for example, as a medium or spiritual healer) or turn them off quite quickly. I will explain how to do this in a seventh chapter.

Causes and development of a kundalini awakening

The big question is this: how does a kundalini awakening come about and why do so few people experience one? We must remember that a kundalini awakening is essentially an expansion of consciousness that initiates or deepens a spiritual development. So, it should be no surprise that it is precisely the desire for personal transformation and expansion of consciousness that is the main trigger for a kundalini awakening. This desire often motivates people to experiment with a wide range of spiritual methods or participate in meditation retreats or workshops. Even for people who had a spontaneous kundalini awakening and had not engaged in spiritual practice, they usually had a desire for personal transformation which caused the expansion of consciousness. What follows are the typical triggers of a kundalini awakening that I have seen in my clients:

Most of my clients experienced a kundalini awakening during an intensive meditation retreat and especially in a silent retreat. Above all, it is the 10-day Goenka Vipassana retreat that I hear most often about. Interestingly, the concept of kundalini is not even recognised in this branch of Buddhism and the teachers on these Vipassana retreats are not at all able to deal with kundalini phenomena. Usually, they simply ask people to leave the retreat if they develop any symptoms. This is, of course, very unfortunate because many of my clients were extremely confused and disappointed by this lack of spiritual support.

The second biggest trigger for a kundalini awakening among my clients are situations where people experience intense feelings of romantic and sexual attraction but do not act on their sexual infatuation. Often these clients believe that the person they have fallen in love with has some form of supernatural, fantastic power that has triggered such an intense experience. But this is not necessarily the case. In my view, it is their strong feelings of infatuation combined with sexual restraint that triggers the awakening.

The third biggest trigger for a kundalini awakening that I have observed in my clients is taking substances such as LSD, cannabis, ayahuasca and magic mushrooms. This has personally surprised me because I believed, just like many other experts in the field, that psychedelic drugs only act temporarily and not long-term. Obviously, I erred in this respect.

The fourth largest trigger is performing general spiritual practices such as meditation, prayer or yoga.

Only a very small number of my clients experienced an awakening through shaktipat (sacred touch) by a spiritual teacher or healer.

Other triggers include living with a partner who has awakened kundalini, near-death experiences and medical interventions such as homeopathy or vaccinations.

Sometimes there is no clear trigger and the person seems to have been born with awakened kundalini.

In my work with over a thousand clients, I have only seen the classic development of kundalini rising as described in Hindu literature in two people. It is a sudden experience of intense energy that begins in the abdomen and then rises chakra by chakra in the spine and then "explodes" in the brain to cause an extremely strong spiritual experience. This experience is often overwhelming and sometimes also accompanied by fears of death but, fortunately, it very rarely happens in this sudden way. The vast majority of my clients develop more kundalini symptoms over a period of a few weeks or months (and in some cases even years) until they meet all the criteria of the kundalini test that I have developed.

The typical course of development of the kundalini process

The development of the kundalini process is very different in different people and depends largely on the psychological, spiritual and overall maturity of a person. For example, Bonnie Greenwell, an American fellow professional of mine, reports that she has primarily been experiencing bliss since her awakening many years ago because she had already spent many years in psychotherapy beforehand and was very open to the concept of shadow work.

On the other hand, I have had many young people as clients who experienced a kundalini awakening after taking drugs and struggled against the idea of having to transform themselves. Instead, they wanted to go back to "partying" again. Generally, one can say that the people who fight the most against this process of expansion of consciousness also have the most long-term problems. By comparison, people who are interested in both personal psychotherapy and spirituality and who do not take themselves so seriously, have the easiest time with this process.

The development of a kundalini process that I have most frequently observed is a first short period of euphoric feelings of perhaps a few weeks or months followed by longer-term challenges in which unpleasant feelings emerge from the subconscious mind and "demand" a proper solution. Those people who humbly and diligently work to resolve these problems one by one will eventually experience bliss along with supernatural abilities. To arrive at this point may take months or, more likely, years depending on how much prior wisdom someone has and how much support they receive.

The expansion of consciousness in the kundalini process is non-reversible and will go on until the end of one's life. For some people, however, this process may also be somewhat in the background and even appear to be dormant again. But this is, in my experience, rarely the case and it only takes another trigger to activate a kundalini influx and revive the process again.

Kundalini Symptoms

Some people may recognise the following list of kundalini symptoms from my first book on kundalini. Unfortunately, I found it impossible to create a new and better list and therefore I will just restate it here.

Mental and spiritual kundalini symptoms
Pleasant symptoms:

Stronger motivation to engage in spiritual practice and spiritual literature

Stronger motivation to make one's lifestyle more loving and more spiritual in every way

Motivation to make eating habits and health care healthier

Strengthened ability to move forward on one`s chosen spiritual path, to understand spiritual literature and to experience exalted states of mind

Motivation to work in a helping profession

Motivation to spend a lot of time in nature and to live in a natural environment

Increased intuition, in-depth wisdom and even clairvoyance

Ability to experience closer contact and communion with one's own higher power

Ingenious insights and increased creativity

Stronger ability to access your subconscious mind and to see your own positive and negative traits in a more realistic manner

Inspiring memories of past lives

Stronger ability to be honest, humble, and laugh at oneself

Increased ability to feel other people's emotions and read their thoughts (this can sometimes be uncomfortable, too)

Increased ability and power to influence and fascinate other people (also called charisma)

Increased ability to manifest one's wishes

Development of supernatural abilities, such as spiritual healing, clairvoyance or telepathy

Hearing heavenly music and sounds

Seeing beautiful lights, sights, visions and colours

Experience of everyday objects and people as extremely aesthetic and beautiful

Reduced material needs and desires

Unpleasant mental and spiritual symptoms:

Increased problems with irrational thinking and confusion such as intensified neurotic thought patterns or erroneous spiritual concepts

Episodes of heightened selfishness, pride or even megalomania (for example, the belief of being Christ)

Episodes of extreme lack of self-confidence

Impulsive decisions based on confused assumptions

Hearing of (frightening) voices and unpleasant sounds

Disturbing memories of childhood or past lives

Seeing terrifying visions, such as distorted faces in the dark, ghosts, demons or torture scenes, etc.

Compulsive thinking

Emotional kundalini symptoms
Pleasant symptoms:

Deep states of bliss and ecstasy

Deep effortless love, forgiveness and compassion towards friends and enemies

Decreased need for emotional support from others

Deep humility, unwavering self-confidence and compassion for oneself and others

Increased motivation and ability to give up negative habits and addictions

Ability to see the inner and outer beauty of human beings and their divine potential

Ability to receive deep emotional support from one`s deity

Unpleasant emotional kundalini symptoms:

Increased negative emotions such as strong fear, despair, depression and anger

Emotions can become so strong that they feel like physical pain

Discovering negative emotions and attitudes that one was previously completely unaware of, such as envy, meanness, racism and hatred

Reinforced guilt feelings

Increased sexual problems

Reliving old emotional traumas and wounds

General hypersensitivity to sensory impressions such as noises, light or simply "vibrations" (for example, when entering a house and finding the atmosphere unbearable)

Fear of becoming mentally insane

Increased relationship problems with family members or friends

Recognising selfish motives in other people (this can also be a positive and empowering experience)

A feeling of alienation from the world

Compulsive symptoms like hand-washing, ruminating etc.

Physical Kundalini symptoms

As explained earlier, most of the following symptoms are not real physical symptoms but symptoms that appear in the body but actually take place in the energy body.

Pleasant symptoms:

Feeling of most pleasant, delicious or orgasmic energy rising from the abdomen or simply in different parts of the body

Better health and resistance to disease (caused by feelings of happiness and a healthier lifestyle - both of which have a positive impact on our immune system)

More beauty, charisma and physical rejuvenation (this happens because of feelings of love and bliss along with a healthier lifestyle that have a positive impact on the ageing process)

Spontaneous ecstatic movements (so-called *kriyas*)

Sexual feelings everywhere in the body (some people find this uncomfortable)

Enormously increased sexual feelings such as strongly intensified orgasms (some people find this uncomfortable)

More physical energy

Unpleasant physical symptoms:

Tingling, buzzing or tickling feelings everywhere in the body

Twitching, shaking or trembling (triggered by strong emotions)

Strange bodily sensations such as a very real feeling that a body part is very enlarged

The reappearance of old chronic pain and illnesses (usually psychosomatic illnesses)

Unexplained short-term pain in many parts of the body: stinging, burning or nagging pain (triggered by emotions that are not recognised as such)

Untreatable chronic pain that is not associated with any diagnosable disease (caused by emotions that are not recognised as such)

A feeling of unpleasant, pushing, pulling or raging energy in the body (triggered by emotions that are not recognised as such)

A feeling that too much energy flows through the body, often through the spine (triggered by emotions that are not recognised as such)

A feeling of energy blockages, such as the experience that energy accumulates in certain areas of the body causing discomfort, pressure or pain (triggered by emotions that are not recognised as such)

Textbook symptoms of commonly known diseases that cannot be found by any physician (triggered by emotions that are not recognised as such)

Hypersensitivity and severe side effects of prescription drugs, alternative medicines, and especially of energetic treatments like acupuncture, homeopathy and hands-on healing

Head pressure

Increased or decreased appetite and need for specific foods

Hot flushes or cold feelings

Unpleasant spontaneous body movements

Unpleasantly increased or decreased libido, embarrassing new sexual desires or a frightening change in sexual orientation

Lack of energy and fatigue (triggered by emotions that are not recognised as such)

Insomnia

Chapter two
Integration of the kundalini process into our lives

One of the most important aspects for alleviating all kundalini symptoms is to accept this process deeply and be willing to integrate it into our lives. In the following sections, I will describe the main areas where this integration should ideally take place.

Acceptance of the kundalini process

Sometimes people have problems accepting that they are in the kundalini process. They desperately want to return to their old personality and fight with a kind of blind rage against all their symptoms. They may, for example, go from doctor to doctor with a hope of receiving a diagnosis for a treatable disease and believe that they could live better that way than accept the fact of having a spiritual awakening and an expansion of consciousness.

Often, these people also develop some kind of self-hatred and accuse themselves of "destroying their lives", of being "abnormally over-sensitive" or simply of being "a loser". I hope it is obvious that these negative attitudes will not serve the integration process in any way. It is, therefore, of the utmost importance to practise compassion and love with ourselves and say to ourselves, "I love myself with all my problems and weaknesses" and imagine being comforted and loved by our higher consciousness.

The process of accepting the kundalini process becomes easier when we realise that we ourselves actually wished for an expansion of consciousness on some level. When I talk to my clients, it almost always becomes obvious that they actively sought to expand their consciousness before their awakening, for example, by participating in a meditation retreat, by reading spiritual books or by taking shamanic substances.

However, it is also true that some people do these things with a partially egotistical motivation, for example, by practising yoga mainly for physical beauty or because they wanted to enhance their personal power through meditation rather than seeking enlightenment for the best of all beings. This is particularly true for people who sought an expansion of consciousness through taking drugs, what I like to call "trying to take an illegal short-cut". These impure motivations lead to painful consequences because the kundalini process mostly makes us feel more vulnerable and humble and not at all superior and independent. Sometimes, people experience this as a kind of "punishment" but that is not how it works. The kundalini process, with all its challenges, is not imposed on us by God or anybody else but happens because of our own desires.

Even if our motivation for a consciousness expansion was not completely pure, we should still acknowledge that at least a part of us really wanted it and that this wish has now been fulfilled. It is only our old ego that is unhappy because it wants to go back to its old convenient numbness and power games which, unfortunately, do not work anymore. In this situation, we should make it clear to ourselves that all this is actually for our benefit because only by letting go of our egotistical motivations can we attain the ultimate liberation. While it may require some work to learn to alleviate our negative emotions and raise our lives to a higher level, it will ultimately be for our benefit and the benefit of the whole world.

A small minority of my clients seem to have experienced a totally spontaneous kundalini awakening - often already in childhood - and without any apparent desire to increase their consciousness. In these cases, I assume that the kundalini rising had already begun in a past life and just continued in this life. In these circumstances too, one should try to accept this process and realise that resistance is just as useless as resisting the awakening of the sex drive in puberty. In both cases, we should understand that our resistance will only create additional problems and that the road to peace consists of channelling both processes into the right direction so that both the kundalini and the sex drive can lead to beautiful happiness.

A further problem in the process of accepting the kundalini process is the possibility of partners, friends or other family members insisting that we must take medication to be "normal" again. In such cases, it is important that we learn to distinguish well-meaning but wrong advice from beneficial advice. Then we should simply refuse to communicate our awakening with people who lack the right understanding.

However, when it comes to our partner, it is important to demand with confidence more understanding and acceptance. Of course, this will only be possible if we ourselves can accept our own awakening first. I will explain in the eighth chapter how to work best with our partner even if they are unwilling to participate in this process of consciousness expansion.

To more easily accept the kundalini process, we should make it clear to ourselves that an expansion of consciousness can be compared to a form of higher intelligence. We are now like a scale, so to speak, that weighs not only kilograms but grams. This means we now have an enlarged supply of data at our disposal, which is a good thing in principle because it allows us to deal more intelligently with the world and with ourselves. If we keep this advantage in mind, it will hopefully make it easier to accept this process.

When a kundalini activation has taken place, it will continue for the rest of our life - just like our sex drive will never completely go away once it has been awakened. This is true even when there are periods in which we hardly ever think about spirituality or sexuality. If the appropriate trigger comes along, these forces will awaken in us once again with all their beauty but also with their challenges. For this reason, we should imagine our first kundalini awakening to be like a gate through which we set out on a lifelong path and we should try not to resist it. Instead, we should bravely face all the challenges on this path and thereby be rewarded with the opportunity to achieve and stabilise a truly higher state of consciousness.

Willingness to let go of one's ego

When I think of all my clients as a group, one of their main commonalities is that they want to be further ahead on the spiritual path than they actually are. Often, they want to be more aloof, more independent, less needy and, especially, less vulnerable than they are. But the kundalini process works in exactly the opposite direction and constantly "rubs our noses" in our all too human weaknesses - in our dependency, neediness and vulnerability.

I was lucky enough to receive many teachings through Tibetan Buddhism that prepared me for this fact. There is, for example, one common statement that *bodhisattvas* (advanced seekers on the spiritual path or what one calls "saints" in Christianity) experience a speck of dust on their hand with the same pain as ordinary people would feel it in their eye. One of my teachers also repeatedly warned us that our hearts would become more sensitive – in fact, like "raw flesh" - and that we should brace ourselves for this pain.

Why do we become needier and more vulnerable on our spiritual path when most people desire nothing more than to be independent and invulnerable? The answer is that independence and invulnerability are the main desires of the ego, thus wanting to deny the true reality of our existence. In Buddhism, there is the teaching of the so-called "Indra's net", which can be thought of as a multidimensional spider's web in which all beings exist as nodes between numerous threads. To be clear, according to this idea, we do not *sit on* one of the many junctions of this net, we literally exist *as the node* that is brought into existence by the many threads that go into it and equally bring other nodes (beings) into existence through threads emerging from it. This means that all beings exist interdependently and that every action and even every thought vibrates through the entire network so that ultimately nothing can be hidden from anyone. However, our ego that strives for autonomy certainly does not want to hear this. Only through the expansion of consciousness during the kundalini process and its resulting pain will we be more or less forced to humbly acknowledge these facts. This process of re-thinking the nature of ourselves and our utter dependence on others needs a long time for many people because we usually want nothing more than to continue striving for independence and invulnerability even if we understand the idea of Indra`s net intellectually. But any attempt to play more of these "ego games" will bring us even more pain in the kundalini process.

Unfortunately, there are many misconceptions and misleading spiritual teachings that promise us quick enlightenment and invulnerability and my clients are regularly disappointed when they realise that these teachings do not work and that they have fallen prey to false gurus and even charlatans. For instance, the common teaching that there is nothing to do but to be "relaxed in the here-and-now" is a complete illusion that our ego is only too happy to believe in the hope of quick enlightenment. Spiritual development is much more than relaxing in the here and now, which is something every little child can do. It is primarily about developing more love, which includes the ability to empathise with other people, the strong desire to help others and includes the humility to acknowledge our many mistakes and weaknesses.

When I state that the kundalini process is "humbling", I certainly do not mean "humiliating". It is more like Socrates said: a truly wise person realises just how little they know. It is the unwise person who believes that they know everything. Through the kundalini process, we experience an expanded consciousness that enables us to recognise our many faults and weaknesses more clearly than before. However, we should always keep in mind that an expansion of consciousness is also a form of higher intelligence that will enable us to find the solutions to many problems, too. This knowledge we can then use to help ourselves and others more effectively.

Letting go of our ego means more than being humble and recognising our weaknesses and dependencies. Tibetan Buddhism teaches that all our suffering results from the belief that our self has an indestructible core that gives us a unique and everlasting identity. This belief will always cause suffering because through the comparison with others, it will always result in arrogance or envy and then feelings of inferiority, anger, depression and anxiety because, unfortunately, we rarely measure up well in these comparisons. Buddhism even goes so far as to say that all suffering, all discord and all war in this world arises from this faulty attachment to the idea of having a unique and indestructible ego.

It is therefore of utmost importance that we recognise that the belief in an ever-lasting and unique essence of ourselves is an illusion and a very pain-inflicting illusion at that. Just like every single cell in our body is

59

regularly renewed and therefore changes our entire body over time, so does our mind consist of many tiny parts which are constantly changing through the varying influences in Indra's net. We can easily recognise this process of change by comparing our current self-image to the one we had 20 years ago or how we were at three years old. I think everyone can admit that they have profoundly changed and that a unique ego-essence is at best only a theory. Instead, we can realise that we are just a potpourri of ever-changing character traits that often also contradict each other. For example, we can be very gentle, spiritual and idealistic but sometimes also behave in a violent, hateful and extremely materialistic way. In Buddhism, these contradictory parts of our mind are called "skandhas", which translates disrespectfully into something like "heap of stuff". This "heap" was created by the many - often contradictory - influences that we have been subjected to in our childhood and exposed ourselves to in adulthood in Indra's network.

If we realise that we do not have a perpetual essence that gives us a unique identity and that we are simply "composed" by a wide range and often contradictory influences (and thus give up our belief in a perpetual, unique self), we will also be able to see that *everything* in us can be changed and improved if we expose ourselves to better and healthier influences. Once we do so, most of our suffering will readily fall away. First of all, our inferiority complexes and envy will disappear because we recognise that there is nothing in us that could not be improved and that we have therefore the opportunity to be anything we want. We just have to look for a role model and learn as much as possible from this person and we will be able to radically change ourselves. For the spiritual path, this means that by uniting with our deity, we can completely give up our old flawed and limited idea of ourselves and ultimately "replace" it with the consciousness of our deity. This is the fastest and easiest way to achieve total enlightenment. On a more ordinary level, letting go of the attachment to our ego means fewer inferiority complexes, envy and competition with other people and thus more empathy and happiness in interpersonal relationships and in our entire life.

Why is giving up our ego attachment so difficult when it supposedly has so many benefits? The answer is that the belief in a unique and everlasting ego is our most profound "thinking mistake" and this false belief works in us like an addiction. Every single form of suffering can be traced back to this misperception. But despite this fact, we stubbornly continue to think in this wrong way just like we continue to eat unhealthy food and indulge in other forms of unwholesome and addictive behaviour. In other words, we behave like little children who just do not want to learn that it would be so much nicer to play harmoniously with other children rather than constantly arguing and wanting all the toys for ourselves. Who can wish with all their heart to unite with their higher power until their self is literally wiped out? In most people, this thought provokes a deep fear and it is this anxiety that is the cause of all our suffering.

The expansion of consciousness in the kundalini process will help us greatly to recognise these dynamics, which are taught by many spiritual teachers in different esoteric schools. But we also need to apply these insights to ourselves and thereby reduce our suffering. Higher-consciousness healing will help us to do just that. It helps us to reduce our ego attachment because it promotes the union with our higher consciousness instead of nurturing the illusion that we can somehow enlighten ourselves as some false spiritual teachings claim. It will also help us to be compassionate with ourselves instead of torturing ourselves through our self-hatred and our envy towards others. The union with the divine and the compassion with ourselves are the first steps towards the loosening of our ego attachment and if we continue on this path, we will one day be able to liberate ourselves from ego attachment altogether.

Relaxing our ego attachment does not mean that we become powerless and allow other people to dominate us. This is a typical trap that many people fall into at the beginning of their spiritual journey. In higher-consciousness healing, we counteract this wrong attitude by always visualising an energy ball around ourselves and around other people. These spheres symbolise the fact that in relationships we also need clear boundaries so that people who are still full of ego attachment cannot dominate us. In this way, we practice the famous Buddhist middle way and will be able to integrate harmoniously the absolute truth of egolessness with the relative truth of healthy ego boundaries. In the fourth chapter, I will explain higher-consciousness healing in detail and how we apply it to our kundalini symptoms.

Integrating our own shadow

I have already mentioned a lot about the fact that it is central in the kundalini process to integrate our shadow, which means the parts of ourselves that we would rather not have. They include primitive aggressions, inappropriate sexual urges and also our traumas and interpersonal conflicts that we prefer to suppress.

Some people who are interested in spirituality are equally interested in psychotherapy and ready to work on their personal history. These people will have the fewest problems in the kundalini process. But there are also quite a lot of spiritual people who hope that practices such as mantra recitation, yoga or shamanistic rituals will automatically dissolve all their psychological problems too, so that they are not required to use any psychological approaches. The kundalini process will, however, put a big spanner into the works. No matter how many mantras we recite or how much yoga we practice, our awakening will vehemently push all our unresolved personal psychological problems into our consciousness and the more we defend ourselves against this process, the more unnecessary complications we will create. For example, the more we try to suppress painful memories with our spiritual practices, the more psycho-somatic problems we may suffer from such as chronic pain or tiredness.

The same pattern applies to our current psychological conflicts with family members or friends. The more we try to "meditate these conflicts away", the more complicated and confusing our kundalini symptoms may become. This dynamic is sometimes referred to as "spiritual bypassing", which means that we try to use spiritual methods to circumvent our psychological problems rather than solve them.

In my work as a kundalini therapist, I would say that perhaps 40% of all my clients' kundalini symptoms are due to unprocessed traumas from the past and around 60% are due to current psychological conflicts. Once these conflicts are acknowledged and resolved with higher-consciousness healing, the kundalini symptoms often fall away as if by magic.

The integration of the shadow side is hardest for those people who believe that they are "a good person". This happens particularly often when people follow a spiritual path that distinguishes strictly between "the good" (the followers of my religion or esoteric group) and "the evil" (the devil, the unbelievers, the critics). These are particularly immature forms of spirituality which sooner or later lead to hypocrisy and all sorts of scandals when it turns out that the priests themselves have not kept to the rules and have committed sinful deeds. A mature spirituality, however, recognises that we always carry loving and selfish tendencies within us at the same time and that it always takes quite a bit of effort and work to separate the two from each other.

It is interesting to see that it is often exactly those who consider themselves to be "good people" who are the ones who hurt others, for example, through angry outbursts, the neglect of their children or even through having affairs. It is not easy to live with the guilt and the shame that arises from doing these things but those who try to suppress or rationalise these feelings away will often experience negative symptoms in the kundalini process such as head pressure.

So, it is important to bravely confront all traumas, interpersonal conflicts and guilt in the kundalini process and willingly work through these rather unpleasant topics. People who actively do shadow work through self-inquiry, psychotherapy or perhaps through art have the easiest time. It is precisely this work that diminishes our egotistical and narcissistic tendencies and makes us more human and compassionate.

Here is an example of how this process might look like in practice: A client of mine was a highly intelligent professor. It was difficult for her to integrate her psychological weaknesses with her high intelligence and impressive career. But she made a lot of effort and told me with great difficulty what kind of "petty" problems she had with her husband. She would have loved to be more tolerant! After her confession, she felt much better and began actively looking for other "petty" problems. She realised that she carried some very vicious misogynist ideas within herself, which was a big shock for her as she considered herself to be an active feminist.

63

She was so ashamed when she told me this but at the same time, she also felt liberated. She had seen herself for a long time as a victim of the patriarchal structures at her university and now saw that she was, in fact, an accomplice. This realisation filled her in equal parts with shame and endless mirth. In her spiritual development, she took a big step forward because she was now able to free herself from her victim role. As a consequence, she experienced the "longest happy time" she had ever experienced in her life.

Handling increased sensitivity

Unfortunately, it is a common misconception that through our spiritual development we will become tougher, more robust and thick-skinned. The opposite is the case! As our spiritual process unfolds, it will become increasingly impossible for us to sweep conflicts under the rug and simply accept things "for the sake of peace". To make matters worse, our environment will often react unfavourably to this development and accuse us of being "over-sensitive" and of "taking things too much to heart".

Our increased sensitivity can also be seen in other areas of life, for instance, our sensory perceptions may appear unpleasantly enhanced. Light may appear too bright, noises too loud, the sun too hot, smells as disgusting, clothes too tight and crowds of people can trigger strong feelings of aversion. Medication - including alternative medicine – can trigger strong side effects and in old houses or churches we may perceive strong "vibrations". Sometimes, we may also feel the feelings of people standing next to us or even perceive the presence of a deceased person.

Our increased sensitivity will also work in a positive sense, for example, by protecting us from wrong decisions because we can now feel more clearly when "something is not right" or when someone has an impure motivation towards us. It will also help us to let go of all sorts of unhealthy behaviours more easily because we can feel and see their negative consequences more clearly than before. Moreover, when it comes to our health, we can use our increased sensitivity to treat many of our illnesses purely through diet or relaxation and thus avoid unpleasant visits to the doctor. We may also experience ordinary joys and pleasures of life as extreme ecstasy and bliss. This applies not only to sexuality but also to the perception of beautiful things or untouched nature. If you meditate regularly, sooner or later you will also experience states of unconditional joy where you experience your entire being as pure bliss. This joy is then the gateway through which you can step in order to attain enlightenment or union with God.

To deal with our sensitivity in the kundalini process in a positive way, we should first of all ban the term "*over-*sensitivity" from our vocabulary and instead confidently speak of our "especially high sensitivity" which enables us to have very high standards in all areas of our life. Of course, we cannot force all the people around us to join us in these high standards. Instead, we should concentrate on finding a place in the world where our sensitivity is an advantage and not a handicap. This can be the case, for example, in many healing or artistic professions, in close relationships with like-minded people and in spiritual groups.

Unfortunately, at the beginning of the awakening process, we will often have to leave some relationships behind to accommodate our heightened sensitivity and perhaps we even have to change our career. All these changes can be stressful but they will help us in the end to create a life in which we feel richly blessed and happy *because* of our sensitivity and not *despite* it.

What will definitely not work is to stubbornly try to be "normal" and to go on as we have done before even though a lot of things in our life do not suit us any longer. For example, if we force ourselves to continue to go to barbecues although we now find the smell of the meat disgusting or if we insist on meeting our old friends in the usual bar even though our friends seem more superficial than before and the bar is much too loud, we are not doing ourselves a favour. Instead, we should try to adapt to our heightened sensitivity rather than fight against it. Therefore, we should always try to surround ourselves with people who we feel good with, instead of trying to be as thick-skinned as we once were. In my personal experience, the latter approach will always be doomed to failure.

If we look at the life stories of many mystics from around the world and throughout history, we can see that most of them have repeatedly withdrawn for extended periods into hermitages, which is a sign that they too needed to deal with increased sensitivity. In the same way, it can sometimes be necessary in the kundalini process to simply stay at home much of the time to experience solitude and silence. When these needs arise, it is important not to fight them and not torment ourselves with thoughts that we have become "neurotic" or have in some way "lost the plot". No, we can congratulate ourselves with a smile that we are now in the illustrious company of the mystics of the world who have always needed a great deal of tranquillity and solitude.

A difficult point in dealing with increased sensitivity is often the relationship with one's partner because, in many cases, the kundalini person has a partner who is not yet as spiritually advanced as they are. I recommend all my clients to try to bring their existing relationship to a higher level rather than to just finish it. We should try to make it clear to ourselves that our partner and children would actually benefit from living at a higher level of consciousness and that they, therefore, should adapt to us and not we to them. My recommendation is to create a so-called tantric relationship with our partner in which we combine the worldly and spiritual aspects of life into a harmonious whole. I will explain the way to do that in the eighth chapter.

There are some visualisation techniques that we can use to protect our senses, such as a protective bubble around ourselves, which I will describe in more detail in the fourth chapter. It will also be helpful to send love to ourselves and all people and situations that are difficult to bear as explained in the same chapter. The most important advice, however, is that we should always carefully observe how things feel and simply let go of everything that has a negative effect on us. Some people will have to change almost their entire life to follow this advice but I still want to encourage everyone to do so because, in my experience, it is the most effective way.

Making our life healthier

In this section, I will probably be writing about a number of things that are familiar to most people because many suggestions about making your life healthier are well known. The problem is that in the kundalini process "too much" can have as many negative consequences as "too little". For example, I have clients who try very hard to eat healthily, take many supplements, go to different healers regularly and visit a new spiritual course every other month. If we go to such an extreme, the medicine – because it is taken in excess – becomes the poison. In the kundalini process, the adage "less is more" applies. So, we should avoid mixing too many health and spiritual measures into a colourful potpourri but use all interventions sparingly – one after the other - and carefully observe our responses.

Nutrition

We should avoid all extremes and regularly consume fresh and wholesome food in balanced quantities. All extremes such as fasting, raw veganism, junk food and extreme low-fat or low-carb diets are not recommended because people in the kundalini process are prone to strong reactions. Many people will want to become vegetarians for ethical reasons, which is very positive but not essential. It is also unnecessary to try to take supplements to influence the kundalini process favourably. It may be good for our health but since the kundalini process is primarily a process of the mind, it is not possible to influence it through extra vitamins or similar things.

An advantage of our strong sensitivity in the kundalini process is that it allows us to use food as a medicine. For example, you can treat bacterial bronchitis with raw garlic, joint inflammation with ginger, menopausal symptoms with soy and stomach pain with turmeric. I myself have solved virtually all the health issues of myself, my family and many of my clients by using this approach and have had many very positive results. There is a literature on this topic and people who are interested in this healing modality should look up the relevant books and websites.

Physical health

In the kundalini process, we should be extremely careful and conservative with all healing procedures. As I have already written, the principle is "less is more" and we should not mix too many healing methods at the same time. Some of my clients, for example, go to a chiropractor, a homeopath and to an acupuncturist simultaneously, which causes even more chaos in their already strained energy body. For this reason, we should only ever use one approach sparingly at a time and closely monitor the effect it has on us. In my experience, people in the kundalini process are not prone to healing crises (which means that it has to get worse before it gets better). Generally, a cure either works quite quickly and clearly or it aggravates our condition and not much in between. Therefore, we should aim at only using those healing methods that have a clear and positive effect on us.

Furthermore, we should be very cautious with all procedures in which we are touched by other people such as massage or hands-on healing. The reason for this warning is that because of our heightened sensitivity, we may pick up unprocessed issues from the healer through the physical contact and thus experience unwelcome side effects. Many of my clients have reported such experiences, as I have too. It is therefore important to only ever work with a therapist who we like as a person and stop the treatment as soon as we get negative symptoms.

All energy therapies, such as homeopathy, acupuncture or reiki, are contra-indicated in the kundalini process. These procedures can lead to particularly serious side effects even though they are generally considered to be very safe. This is because these energy healing methods have been developed for people who are not in the kundalini process. They are meant to help the flow of energy in patients or – in the way I express it – start the melting process of the ice and open the subconscious mind. But if we already have too much melted ice, we need help to calm the wildly raging water down (our out-of-control emotions) and do not need remedies that bring even more material to the surface. If someone in the kundalini process wants to try these methods, I would recommend proceeding with caution and stopping the treatment immediately if they feel worse.

Furthermore, all breathing techniques should be avoided in the kundalini process as they can have very serious side effects - just like energy treatments. I once had a client, for example, who suffered from chronic heart palpitations, which disappeared as soon as he stopped the breathing exercises he had diligently practised and instead used the anti-anxiety breathing technique that I teach. Another client reported long-lasting panic attacks after practising the continuous (over-)breathing that is used in re-birthing.

Breathing exercises have a very strong influence on our body and mind and should, in my opinion, be individually "prescribed" by a qualified breathing-therapist in order to have a positive effect. Unfortunately, it is common practice nowadays that in yoga or qigong groups the whole group is guided to breathe in the same way and thereby ignore the fact that different people need very different breathing interventions. Fast techniques like fire breathing can work as a poison in anxious and over-excited people while techniques such as the continuous breathing as in re-birthing can trigger catastrophic effects in sensitive kundalini people, which may last for weeks or even longer. In this book, I am going to introduce one single breathing technique (the anti-anxiety breathing technique) that I have used with great success in many thousands of therapy sessions and which has never amplified any kundalini problems afterwards.

Psychedelic drugs such as cannabis, LSD and magic mushrooms are to be strictly avoided as they can trigger psychosis in people with or without kundalini. This also applies to shamanic substances such as Ayahuasca, which are currently very fashionable. I have had several kundalini clients who had experienced extreme and long-lasting anxiety and even psychosis after participating in (supposedly safe) Ayahuasca ceremonies.

People who need to take prescription drugs should take them as sparingly as their disease allows and should reduce their medication only after consulting their doctor. This applies especially for medication given for mental issues. If someone has taken these medications for a long time, they often get out of the practice of handling strong negative emotions and therefore it is important to taper those medications off very slowly - and only with the support of the attending health care provider and, if possible, in agreement with close family members.

69

Moreover, one should not underestimate the significant placebo effect when taking medications, which act as a strong crutch in addition to the chemistry of the pills. It would be very unwise to take this crutch away too quickly.

After these warnings about the rapid discontinuation of psychiatric drugs, I would like to point out that there are large scientific studies, such as those from Irving Kirsch, which show through a meta-analysis of all existing studies that anti-depressants do not work any better than placebo. This naturally raises the question of why they are still prescribed since they also have many harmful side effects. I would also like to point out that anti-psychotic drugs have no place in the kundalini process unless a person is simultaneously schizophrenic or bipolar. But I have often heard from my clients that they were given diagnoses such as "semi-psychotic" or "psychosis-like" and were then medicated as if they had real schizophrenia even though they never suffered an actual loss of sanity.

In this context, it is also important to know that no one can be forced to take psychiatric drugs against their will or to go to psychiatry unless there is an acute self-endangerment such as suicide or the threat of violence against other people. Also, one cannot be sectioned just by a doctor, let alone by family members, but only through a judge who is specialised for such cases. So, the fear that parents or a partner could force us to go to psychiatry is unwarranted because it is impossible under the existing legislation in Western countries.

Despite these facts, my advice is not to try to speak to doctors or psychiatrists about the kundalini or spiritual awakening. Since this concept is not widely known, it can be easily misunderstood. You should also avoid speaking about unwanted paranormal experiences since you could get easily be labelled as being psychotic or even schizophrenic. I had a number of clients who received such diagnoses. I spoke to them in detail about their experiences and in most cases, there was neither a loss of reality nor an impairment of functioning in everyday life, which means that these diagnoses had not been warranted. However, it is not easy to get rid of such a label once it has been stuck on someone and it will be an additional burden in an already challenging process.

It is, of course, always advisable to go to a doctor to get checked out if severe physical symptoms are present. In the conversations with a health care provider, I advise to only speak of "ordinary" physical and psychological symptoms such as pain, anxiety or tiredness. Once you are told that you are physically healthy, you can then work with the methods in this book to get better quickly.

Sexuality

In all areas of life, it is important to find a happy medium between extremes and this applies to the area of sexuality as well by avoiding the extremes of celibacy and promiscuity. Again and again, I have had clients who somehow believed that it would benefit their spiritual path if they were sexually abstemious and who forbade themselves to masturbate. In most cases, however, the opposite is true. Their repressed sexuality and lack of orgasms only reinforced all unpleasant kundalini symptoms and increased their neurotic fears about the "sinfulness" of masturbation and the like.

Over the last hundred years, the oppressive Christian sexual morality in the Western world has greatly eased and at the same time the so-called hysterical symptoms (conversion symptoms), of which Sigmund Freud wrote so much, have greatly reduced. So, it makes little sense to revive these obsolete concepts by replacing them with some sexual suppression theories from Asia. This is especially important to understand for people who experience a strong increase in sexual feelings during the kundalini process, which frequently happens in the early stages of an awakening.

To deal with our sexuality positively, we should remember that the kundalini process is about the union of the upper and lower chakras - or in other words, the union of sexuality (or power) and love. We can, therefore, describe our most profound suffering as our striving for power, aggression and sexuality in our lower chakras being in direct contradiction with the need for love in our heart and the ideals in our head. We can see this inner rupture clearly when we find someone sexually attractive but know that they would be really bad for our heart. Or the other way around, we know a very nice person but, unfortunately, we do not find them sexy enough to fall in love with. Some people also suffer because their sexual preferences are completely out of harmony with their spiritual ideals or they do sexual things that they later regret, such as having affairs or watching pornography. In my experience, for most people, it is not at all easy to bring their sexual needs into perfect harmony with the needs of their heart except in the first phase of falling in love with someone. So, our goal should be to heal this fundamental contradiction between our sexuality and our heart and avoid all activities that could deepen it.

Masturbation is important and healthy as I already have described but one should not do it extremely often and it is also essential to avoid pornography. One might hope that spiritual people would know this but, unfortunately, this is not at all the case. Almost all of my male clients regularly watch pornography, which can have disastrous consequences for the sensitive mind of a person in the kundalini process. There is already a lot of information available about the negative psychological impacts of watching pornography and if someone has problems to stop this, they should inform themselves about these impacts. In short, pornography can cause impotence, feelings of guilt and anxiety, weaken self-esteem and can cause problems in relationships, especially in love relationships. And then there is the moral component that a number of female pornography actresses are victims of human trafficking or modern-day slavery. So, if you look at pornography, you can never be sure that you are not watching the real rape of underage girls and thus making yourself an accomplice.

To grow spiritually and to unite our hearts and sexuality, we should also avoid all other activities that deepen our inner rupture such as one-night stands or so-called tantric massages. Some of my male clients have told me about the great joys of these massages. However, it is a fact that during these massages the heart connection between the masseuse and the client is unimportant. So, it should come as no surprise that these men's marriages became worse as a result of their activities and that their inner conflicts were deepened rather than being healed.

Some people experience in the kundalini process a complete cessation of their sex drive. As long as there are no problems with their partner and no chronic medical issues or fatigue, we can be satisfied about this because it means that our entire sexual energy has now been channelled into the kundalini and mind expansion process. This is a positive development but we should never try to force it because, especially among young people, it is extremely rare and there is a danger that we inadvertently suppress our sexual energy.

Anyone who has sexual desire should always try to channel it into a loving relationship and make sure that during sex the lust of the genitals gets thoroughly mixed up with the loving embrace of the heart. Whoever "makes love" like that will achieve the union of the lower and upper chakras much faster and the sex with their beloved partner will be a "spiritual highway" towards enlightenment. In the eighth chapter, I have written more about how to work with tantric sex and solve other problems around sexuality in the kundalini process.

Living our life according to the highest moral principles

Nowadays the word "morality" has almost gone out of fashion. But we cannot afford this nonchalance when we go through a spiritual awakening. I've seen in myself and also heard from many clients that often the slightest moral misconduct immediately comes back to us like a boomerang. This corresponds with the Tibetan Buddhist teaching that explains that through intensive spiritual practice our "negative karma ripens much faster" and that we, therefore, experience more "challenges" or "purifications". I cannot say whether this fact applies to every person in the kundalini process because, as I mentioned before, some people abuse this process for their self-interest. But a number of clients have reported that this effect was happening for them.

Morality and ethics are very important in the spiritual process and are often neglected in current New Age literature. The indirect message from New Age teachers is that moral decisions are so simple and obvious that one does not even have to mention them. However, in my experience, moral decisions are anything but easy and I can see with my clients on a daily basis how much suffering they experience because they cannot recognise and name immoral behaviour in others and therefore find it difficult to defend themselves against it. Sometimes, they do not recognise

73

their own moral misconduct either and create even more problems in that way.

I have mentioned before that in Tibetan Buddhism we have the beautiful picture that a successful spiritual development is like a house. The foundation is ethical behaviour, the walls are love and the roof is the recognition of our true nature. We can see from this image that without a strong ethical foundation, all our other spiritual efforts will be in vain because the walls of love and the roof of knowledge have no support. Unfortunately, there are many spiritual movements these days that focus only on the "roof," such as Neo-Advaita. These teachings are not wrong but unfortunately incomplete and therefore cannot be effective.

Moral misbehaviour involves everything that does not follow the beautiful saying, "Do unto others as you would be done by". This applies only to words and actions and not to all the ugly impulses and thoughts that we may discover in our minds. The latter we can just let pass by, or better yet, make some good-natured jokes about them. In this way, we can use self-deprecating humour to turn our ugliness into joy, which is in keeping with the kundalini transformation process.

Even people who generally do the right thing and are not guilty of any major misdeed often behave in morally wrong ways in their partner relationships and families. This could be finer or coarser forms of selfishness, failure to help others and, especially, overlook and therefore strengthen the moral misconduct of others. If our partner or children aggressively talk to us, tell little lies or do other selfish things, is it better to make these things into an issue or should we let others get away with these behaviours for the sake of the peace? To grow spiritually, I would say it is generally better to confront all selfish behaviours but, of course, it always depends on the individual case.

Another problem area is how we earn our living. If you have acquired healing or clairvoyant abilities, it is tempting to want to earn money from it. I think, however, this would carry a high ethical risk because these supernatural skills often come and go and we would receive money from our clients even on bad days when we know that we do not have access to our gifts. I think it would be much wiser to finish a proper qualification such as a naturopath, masseur or psychotherapist and then to charge only for this work. If someone has supernatural powers, they can add them as a gift for free. I deal with my clairvoyant abilities in this way and therefore I am never tempted to make clairvoyant statements when my intuition is not in peak form.

Generally speaking, in the kundalini process, everyone will have to deal thoroughly with the moral dimension of their own behaviour and that of others sooner or later. The expansion of consciousness will not allow people to continue sweeping these things under the rug as they may have done before their awakening.

Finally, I would like to stress that in our efforts to make our lives morally impeccable, we should not forget the Buddhist middle path. There is, unfortunately, no chance of living our life with complete nonviolence and honesty. It starts with the fact that our white blood cells are constantly killing invading pathogens and even the strictest vegan diet does, unfortunately, involve the killing of numerous living beings during the growing and preparation of vegetables. Furthermore, in the name of diplomacy and courtesy one should not always tell the truth because brutal honesty will often create unnecessary suffering. We should use our best conscience to strive for the highest moral perfection but without going into any extreme.

Seeing our environment as a mirror

Our increasing awareness and sensitivity in the kundalini process can sometimes make us feel overwhelmed by the problems of everyday life. For example, some of my clients have told me that this world sometimes appears to them as a kind of hell realm or that God appears to them to be a sadistic creature who enjoys playing cruel games with them. Other clients find this world just unbearable. Unfortunately, this kind of thinking makes them into helpless victims and causes depression and despair.

According to the Buddhist point of view, we are the creators of our environment and what we see around us is a reflection of our inner beliefs and attitudes. We can imagine that the six main chakras that lay along our central channel in the middle of our body look like movie projectors and the world around us is like a multidimensional screen onto which our film is projected. Each chakra is responsible for one of the six main areas of our life through the attitudes that we hold within it.

The root chakra is responsible for our body and how comfortable and confident we feel within it and how much we can enjoy earthly pleasures like sex, sports or dancing. The navel chakra is responsible for how much power we have and, for example, how much money we can earn from our work. The solar plexus chakra stands for bonding, emotional security, peace and harmony. It generates either a feeling of calm and peace or a sense of a world in which we have to be constantly afraid and worried. Through the heart chakra, we create the quality of our love relationships and through the throat chakra, the quality of our communication and whether all give and take in our life is fair or not. The head chakra is in charge of our world view including our spirituality and our ability to see things constructively or become depressed and confused.

It is not always easy to see that we have created our environment when we are in a very painful phase and we may become outraged when someone comes along and suggests that we have created our suffering. But we should at least try to recognise that our ignorance has fundamentally contributed to our problems. For example, nobody gets married to get divorced and yet half of all married people find themselves in that predicament. It is our unawareness that did not allow us to see the early warning signs at the beginning of the relationship that could have told us that the relationship has no chance of survival.

In order to see our environment as a mirror, it is helpful if we accept the concept of reincarnation and that in our past lives we have unconsciously made many decisions that have now led to our problems. This is not the same as the popular New Age idea that we have consciously chosen our problems in order "to teach ourselves a lesson". Such thinking would just be cruel. No, all our problems have come solely from our ignorance, just as our unawareness has caused us to slide into a bad marriage that we could have avoided if had not ignored the early warning signs.

Although we may not always be able to understand how and why we have created our problems, it will still be very helpful if we can accept this concept at least theoretically. As soon as we do this, we hold the key in our hand to radically change not only ourselves but also our environment. To do that, we have to do more than just thinking positively. It is necessary to go with our attention directly into the relevant chakra and let go of all our negative feelings and images and replace them with positive ones. We do this by practising higher-consciousness healing which I have described in the fourth chapter. These techniques are also described in more detail in my book *Advanced Manifesting*.

For the healing of kundalini symptoms as well as for the manifestation of our dreams, the same maxim applies: Chakra change means life change! This truth cannot be emphasised enough and offers the key to radically transform ourselves and our environment into something much more positive.

Living with awakened awareness in an un-awakened world

I will not lie about it – it is not always easy to live with an awakening awareness in a largely un-awakened world. But it certainly does not have to be the horror trip that many people see in a kundalini awakening. A very painful account, for example, comes from Gopi Krishna who made the topic of kundalini famous with his books in the 1980s. He created a lot of unnecessary suffering for himself through his refusal to seek out a spiritual teacher. He also focused much too much on his negative symptoms, which greatly intensified them. Moreover, every time he had a new kundalini influx, he stopped eating and almost starved himself to death. All such problems and complications do not need to happen if the kundalini process is better understood and if we apply the appropriate methods to alleviate our unpleasant symptoms.

My own life has only become better and more beautiful under the influence of this force and I have been living for almost 20 years with a constant feeling of deep bliss that even continues more or less when negative things happen to me. Also, the external circumstances of my life, such as my marriage, my general health, work and housing situation have only ever improved.

Through the kundalini process, we have the potential to manifest the highest spiritual happiness in all relationships and circumstances of our life in a very tangible way and become an even greater help to other people. To achieve this, we need to adopt the attitudes described in this chapter and practise the techniques I will describe later. If we take this advice to heart and devote our lives to our spiritual development, we will surely be able to reap the enormous fruits that are waiting for us on this amazing journey of expansion of consciousness.

But until we can manifest our personal life as a paradise, most of us will have to spend some time as a kind of outsider in an un-awakened and sometimes unbearably rough world. It is a world of lies in which our wish to be authentic is often met with rejection or even hatred. Our desires for more love and health are mocked and our expanded awareness is often dismissed as nonsense or even as a form of mental illness.

My most important piece of advice in the face of all these challenges is to make compassion the most important part of one's spiritual practice. It is the only way to live in peace with people who simply cannot understand our expanded consciousness because it is not accessible to them and makes them afraid. Compassion is also the only way to forgive people who attack us when our very existence confronts them with truths that make them feel angry and envious.

Secondly, we should try to find a spiritual group that can be like a kind of family for us and where we do not need to be an outsider any longer. I recommend a group with a long tradition because I think such groups are safer than those around any self-announced spiritual teachers who have not been qualified by anyone. When choosing a teacher, one should not be too impressed by the number of students that a guru has attracted because true spirituality cannot necessarily be quantified by how many followers someone has. Instead, I recommend visiting several spiritual groups and seeing where you feel most comfortable. It is also advisable to use the Internet to find out whether a potential teacher has been involved in any scandals. It is wise to stay away from gurus who have questionable morals and not fall for the rationalisations that their devoted followers use to sanctify their teacher's immoral behaviour. In the eighth chapter, I have given a more detailed explanation about how to recognise a good spiritual teacher.

Unfortunately, in many spiritual groups, we may encounter incomprehension about the kundalini process. A simple way to find out if a teacher has had a kundalini awakening themselves is to request a private conversation and ask how they deal with bliss and paranormal experiences. By observing the tone of voice and body language, one can quickly ascertain if he or she has had such experiences or not. We don't have to have a teacher who has had a kundalini awakening themselves but it would, of course, be beneficial. However, if you notice that a teacher is afraid of a kundalini awakening or even rejects it as a kind of "devil's work", you should look for another group as soon as possible. It is important not to give up too quickly but to continue your search until you have found a group in which you feel at home.

There is no need to spend much time with your spiritual group if you are going through a phase where you need a lot of solitude and seclusion. It is more about the feeling of having a spiritual family because I do not think that we as human beings ever leave this need entirely behind.

Some people in the kundalini process make the mistake of naively assuming that all other people are on the same level of consciousness as they are themselves are or even more highly developed. I made that mistake for a long time, which happened probably because this process started in me at an age when I was still almost a child. As a young person, I always had the feeling that other people lived by rules of a game that I simply did not understand and that no one wanted to explain these rules to me.

Today, I can see, of course, that these were the rules of the ego games that most people play to climb up their imaginary pecking order to elevate themselves at the expense of others. Due to the humbling influence of the kundalini process, I have never really been able to participate in such games and was instead greatly confused by the "strange" behaviour of others that I simply could not understand. That caused me a lot of suffering back then because in my confusion I often felt inferior to others. Now, of course, I can see that it was actually to my advantage that my fate had closed off to me the spiritually dead-end road of ego games. I am telling this story to encourage everyone to adopt an attitude that our kundalini problems are beneficial spiritually because they accelerate our understanding and motivation to turn towards the only truly important thing, namely, the union with the divine.

It is also important that we have at least one person in our lives with whom we can speak openly about our spiritual experiences. This can be our partner, a friend or a spiritual teacher. The main thing is that we do not have to bottle these experiences up within ourselves but that we have regular exchanges about them with a sympathetic person.

When it comes to the rest of the world, we should keep our experiences on the kundalini path as secret as possible so that we do not attract negative reactions such as fear, misleading advice or envy. In Tibetan Buddhism, the kundalini path is known as the tantric or secret path. It is called secret because it is supposed to be kept secret since there is also a danger of using it as an ego trip or even creating a two-tier society (i.e. "we with the awesome kundalini awakening and you who do not have a clue"). Therefore, we should not tell anyone but our most intimate confidants of things like visions, ecstasies, kriyas (involuntary body movements) or supernatural powers.

Once we have become far advanced on our kundalini path, there will at some point come a time when we can no longer keep our abilities a secret and when our environment will recognise us as a being of great beauty, full of blissful feelings and incredible powers. We then face the challenge of dealing with the temptation of self-aggrandisement as well as with the envy and the furious attacks that this development is bound to provoke. The keywords in this situation are, as before, "humility" and "compassion".

The higher we soar into spiritually blissful worlds, the more compassion we need to deal with the relentless ego-attacks from the people who are still attached to their animalistic pecking order thinking and who just cannot stand the idea that other people have something that makes them seem inferior. Likewise, we need ongoing humility to resist all of our megalomaniac temptations. If you read the biographies of famous saints in many spiritual traditions around the world, you can see that many of them went through phases of difficult temptations and that, unfortunately, a number of them could not resist the trap of megalomania.

The final development of a kundalini awakening also brings the possibility of helping other people more effectively and the joy and satisfaction that comes from this work will make all the egotistical envy of other people seem rather unimportant. I suppose that for most people such a development will take place only after decades of dedicated spiritual work or even in future incarnations.

To end this chapter, I want to reiterate how important it is that we keep our kundalini experiences mostly to ourselves.

Chapter three
Walking the middle path

To master the kundalini process, it is of paramount importance to avoid all extremes and find the famous Buddhist middle way. This balance between two opposing poles is so important that it represents one of the most central teachings of Buddhism and this view is also absolutely central for mastering the kundalini process in the best way possible. For all those who do not know the origin of the teaching of the middle way, I will briefly summarise it here.

When the Buddha was not yet a Buddha, his name was Siddhartha Gautama and he lived as a prince about 2,500 years ago in an Indian palace in extreme luxury. All sights of suffering were kept away from him until he secretly left the palace as a young man and for the first time, encountered sights of poverty, illness and death. The shock of seeing this suffering elicited in him the desire to embark on a spiritual path and he began with a discipline of extreme asceticism which was common in those days. He almost starved himself to death until one day it became clear to him that this exaggerated self-mortification was a spiritual dead-end road. He realised that we can only make the greatest spiritual progress if we can find a balance between self-discipline and letting go and illustrated this with the image of a well-tuned violin string. An overly tight string will break and a string that is too loose will not produce any sound. In the same way, we develop in the best way on a middle path between the extremes of self-mortification and complacency.

The teaching of the middle path is never more important than in the kundalini process because our energy and feeling system responds extremely sensitively to even the mildest imbalances in all areas of our life. Walking the middle path, however, does not mean finding a tepid average between the opposites but involves living both extremes *simultaneously and to a maximum*. This is easier than it sounds. For example, if we take the pairing of surrender and control, the middle ground does not mean "a little" control and "a little" surrender but maximum control combined with maximum surrender. A real-life example of such an attitude would be a female tango dancer who unites in herself perfect body control with a maximum surrender to her partner.

When it comes to the opposites of power and love, we should try to combine a maximum of love with a maximum of power. This can easily be illustrated through the example of bringing up children: it is not enough to give our children "a little bit of love" and to "keep them a little bit" away from walking onto a busy road. No, most parents will agree that we should love our children with all our heart and simultaneously stop them (at least when they are small) with all our power from harming themselves.

Why is the middle ground so important? The Taoist teaching of yin and yang teaches us that every extreme will be forced into its opposite if we go too far into it. For example, if we work too long and too much (yang), then we will experience a burn-out at some point and be forced into complete passivity (yin). And if we try too long to be patient (yin), we will, at some point, have an enormous outburst of anger (yang). In other words, no matter what spiritual teaching or method we use, if we use it excessively, the medicine becomes poison. In my counselling practice, I see every day that almost all my clients are prone to go into some extremes and through the resulting imbalance they produce many avoidable kundalini symptoms. The aim, therefore, is to stop swinging between the extremes and instead find a way to unite all opposites into a harmonious whole.

The rest of this chapter describes typical extreme attitudes which I have repeatedly observed in my clients and which we should try to correct in order to avoid kundalini symptoms. The pairs of opposites that I describe overlap in part and the list is not necessarily exhaustive.

Control versus surrender

Almost all of my clients have a great deal of resistance to exercising more control over their minds and other people and believe that more letting go and surrendering is the answer to all their problems. The opposite, however, is usually the case because it is very often the excessive surrender that worsens many kundalini symptoms. You can find the excessive desire for surrender in many popular expressions, which are quite negative in the kundalini process when used in excess, such as, "just let it happen"; "just let go into this process"; "just surrender to the kundalini"; "just accept it" or "just relax".

When we think of our ice-block metaphor, it is easy to see why excessive surrender is not beneficial. Surrender accelerates the melting process of our ice-block and transforms it into raging water (uncontrollable emotions) which floods all our inner dams. It is much more advantageous that the melting process (the expansion of consciousness) works slowly in a dribbling way so that we have enough time to handle and integrate the emerging material. Therefore, most of my clients need more control to bring their over-surrender back into balance. The guiding sentences should ideally look like this:

*Inform yourself thoroughly so that you do not get scared in this process. Use skilful methods to alleviate your negative emotions. Try to use humour to deal with your lower impulses. Keep your body in an upright posture and keep your eyes open so that you stay in control. Tense your muscles to control your involuntary body movements so they do not control you. **AND** accept the consciousness expansion process, relax and do not exhaust yourself in futile struggles against this process.*

Of course, we should not go to the other extreme of over-control and useless fighting against the kundalini process, either. I see this behaviour much less often in my clients and, as a group, they have more of a tendency towards over-surrender. I explain this with the fact that teachings on letting go and surrender are over-emphasised in most spiritual books, meditation classes or yoga groups. This makes perfect sense because surrender will jump-start the kundalini process. However, once the consciousness expansion process has begun in earnest, we need more control or skilful methods to master it.

Helping oneself as opposed to relying on God

As a group, my clients tend to expect help from God instead of helping themselves. I see this often in expressions like, "God wants me ... "; "it is

84

not meant to be"; "let go, let God"; "I will be punished (by God)"; "I am tested (by God)" or in questions like, "why does God let these things happen?" or "why doesn't God help me?" Some clients are also really angry at God because he does not help them.

I explain to my clients that a single glance at a newspaper confirms that God does not help good people. My clients are therefore often stuck in some sort of childhood faith that God will reward the good children and help them. Unfortunately, this naive belief fails the test of reality and the kundalini process painfully confronts us with our naivety.

According to Tibetan Buddhism, a deity is a being that loves us like a mother or a father loves their only child but who cannot (and should not) do our homework for us. In other words, we can look to these deities as role models and we can also receive their love. Nevertheless, we have to solve our problems by ourselves. This becomes easier if we are willing to learn from our higher power and accept their loving consolation.

According to Tibetan Buddhism, a deity has neither created the world nor do they interfere with our life - as many Christians believe - but we ourselves have created our own destinies through our own actions in many incarnations. We, therefore, do not need to be angry at God because he allows our suffering but we ourselves should try to take responsibility for everything in our lives – good and bad.

If we relate in this way to our higher power, we will unite the opposite pair: reliance on a higher power and helping ourselves. We also combine the pair of opposites: to do God's will and follow our own free will into a harmonious whole.

Caution versus trust

As a group, my clients tend to be too trusting and thus get themselves into many difficulties that could be easily avoided. This behaviour is especially noticeable when it comes to my clients' willingness to follow dubious spiritual teachers without examining them properly. I have even seen highly successful lawyers, scientists and doctors throwing caution to the wind who would never allow themselves to be fooled in this way in their workplace. But when it comes to spirituality, they sometimes behave very naively and seem to leave their critical faculties at the front door of an ashram or spiritual centre.

Many of my clients also believe that every spiritual book that has become a bestseller must be of true spiritual value. Unfortunately, this is not at all the case but rather a sign that an author was able to write exactly what the majority of people at a certain time in history wanted to read. Nowadays, most people do not want to hear how difficult it is to reach enlightenment but rather how extremely easy it is.

A number of my clients also have spiritual teachers who publicly engage in addictive behaviours, exploit women or are even convicted paedophiles. Often, my clients rationalise these behaviours with concepts like "crazy wisdom" or they find other "explanations" to minimise the significance of these things. It does not seem to worry them that their teacher's destructive attitudes could rub off on them and may lead to diminished self-confidence in women, for example, or increased chauvinism among men.

I sometimes see the same overly trusting attitude when it comes to internal paranormal phenomena. Some clients, for example, want to befriend the demons that they experience. My response is that they are like a child lost in a big city and stranded in a red-light district that is full of dubious characters. It simply would not be wise to approach strangers in such a situation and I advise them to be cautious.

Of course, we should not be over-cautious either and stop trying anything. With the right kind of security measures, it is possible to safely talk to a demon in the paranormal world. But we should not be too surprised if it attacks us and we should know how to proceed in such a situation. I will explain how to do this in the seventh chapter. In this section, I would just like to stress the need for being more critical without being overly cautious.

Rational thinking versus intuition

As a group, my clients tend to give intuition priority over rational thinking. Unfortunately, this preference can have difficult consequences because decisions based on faulty intuition often have far more extreme consequences than mistakes based on faulty rational thinking. An example would be how we invest our money. Through a rational misjudgement after checking all the facts, we may lose a small amount of money. However, if we wrongly invest a large amount of money based on nothing but an intuitive hunch, we may lose all of it.

Another example is how people choose their spiritual teachers. If we only use our intuition, we can easily end up in the clutches of a charlatan because these people are very skilled in manipulating potential students. It would be much better to use both the intelligence of our heart (intuition) *and* the intelligence of our head (rationality) to make such decisions. Therefore, we should not just follow our enthusiastic feelings but also take into account the facts about a potential teacher that can be found on the internet. Irrational thinking will create many problems in the kundalini process because the process does not allow us to "rationalise away" the "unusual" behaviour of famous spiritual teachers as is so often done. Instead, our heightened sensibility will "rub our noses" into all our thinking mistakes until we become more sensible.

Of course, all this does not mean that we should neglect our intuition altogether. On the contrary, the kundalini process offers us a unique opportunity to develop this ability to a high degree. I myself have developed many clairvoyant abilities but it has taken me many years of a very structured – and therefore rational – approach to develop them properly. I recommend to everyone to proceed in the same way because intuitions feel exactly like every other illusion or crazy idea and it is almost impossible to tell the difference between these mental impressions. Only after many years of experience can we claim with a certain degree of certainty that we are mostly right with our hunches. But even then, we can never be sure.

To sharpen our intuition, we should try to think of many tests so that we can check its accuracy. I myself, for example, wrote down for over ten years thousands of intuitions and then checked if there were any contradictions among them, whether I may have received the information from other sources and whether the predictions came true. When I did aura-readings, I always asked for feedback about how accurate they were. After ten years, I concluded that my success rate was about 90%. So, I know that I can always be wrong and that is why I always continue to use my rational mind to check my intuitions. My error rate is highest when it comes to my desires and I have had to bury quite a few crazy ideas in the graveyard of "false intuitions". So, I also advise all my clients to be humble in this area and always use both halves of their brain - the intuitive and the rational hemispheres.

Planning the future versus being in the now

With this pair of opposites, my clients as a group tend to value the here-and-now higher than planning the future. My clients also often have an aversion against thinking about the past and we can include this here, as well.

Unfortunately, trying to be in the here-and-now can have far more negative consequences than over-planning the future or too much ruminating about the past. It is precisely our ability to imagine the consequences of our actions that prevents endless amounts of suffering, especially when it comes to avoiding addictive behaviour. In the same way, the analysis of our past mistakes can accelerate our personal development because we can learn from our missteps, rather than constantly repeating them.

But many of my clients have the idealistic idea that simply staying in the here-and-now will solve all their problems. Unfortunately, it is exactly those people who can be more easily exploited and dominated both by unscrupulous spiritual teachers as well as by their partners.

Those who worry too much about the future or are depressed because they ruminate too much about their past traumas will find much relief from meditation in which they rest their mind in the present moment. In that way, they can discover that the present moment has a lot of happiness to offer.

Ideally, we should learn to combine the analysis of the past, the resting in the here-and-now and the planning of the future into a harmonious whole and not overemphasise one at the expense of the other two.

Making judgments versus acceptance

I cannot count how many of my clients believe that it is "spiritually wrong" or even "sinful" to make judgments. Unfortunately, they do not realise that this attitude can easily make them into victims of selfish and exploitative people. My clients are often even more shocked when I explain to them that overemphasising acceptance is actually promoting evil in other people simply because they are allowing it.

Those who want to grow spiritually and control their kundalini symptoms cannot afford to shy away from judgments and even sharp condemnations. We need to be able to say "these spiritual instructions are *fundamentally wrong*" or "this spiritual teacher has sexually abused women, which I *condemn*" or "my partner takes advantage of me and *that is wrong* and the fact that he had a difficult childhood does not excuse his behaviour in any way." Anyone unwilling to think in this way not only makes themselves easily into a victim but also can become an accomplice because they allow the dominating and even exploitative behaviour of others.

Of course, we do not want to turn to the opposite and constantly, aggressively attack everything that we do not approve of. That is why we must always express our judgments with compassion and kindness. Nor should we lose sight of the fundamental truth that all human beings have a divine nature and that all suffering in the world comes from our basic ignorance. This insight helps us to have a certain amount of patience and tolerance.

Ultimately, the most important thing is to find a place in the world where we can best contribute to reducing the suffering of all beings. We will only succeed in doing this if we can combine our willingness to accept things as they are with our critical attitude into a harmonious whole.

Making changes in the outside world versus turning inside and meditating

As a group, my clients are more inclined to solve their problems through meditation and psychotherapy than by making changes in the outside world. They often argue that they would first like to get themselves in order before they interact with others in relationships or at work. When this pair of opposites is out of balance sometimes extreme cases occur whereby people just stay at home, withdraw from all relationships and no longer participate in normal life. (I am not talking about people who are sick.)

In rare cases, such a retreat from the world may be useful for a short time but mostly I advise my clients to combine their inner work with outer work. For example, if someone suffers from social anxiety, they will not get better just by retreating and meditating a lot. The anti-anxiety exercise that I will explain in the fifth chapter should be associated with facing one's anxiety in many social situations. It is also unlikely to find one's dream job only by going on meditation retreats. In such a case, it would be better to take up some internships in conjunction with visualising a workplace that fulfils all one's criteria.

For the reasons I have just explained, I'm not necessarily a proponent of long meditation retreats. I personally know about a dozen people who graduated from Tibetan Buddhist three-year retreats and the results did not convince me. A surprisingly large number of them turned away from Buddhism, which is a confirmation of the theory that extreme behaviours often turn almost compulsively into their opposites. It is, therefore, also true that the harmonisation of inner and outer work brings us faster to our goal than swinging back and forth between extremes.

Negative thinking as opposed to positive thinking

Another pair of opposites is positive thinking and negative thinking. As a group, my clients have a strong preference to think positively and reject so-called negative thinking. This often leads to a phenomenon called "spiritual bypassing". This term means that we use spiritual methods to avoid recognising our dissatisfaction and to suppress our emotions. My clients say, for example: "Yes, I had a bad childhood/marriage/divorce but I have forgiven them all and the subject is done for me" or, "I know that no one is really a victim, so I will not complain" or "I shouldn't grieve for my dead mother, it's all just attachment."

These statements are too extreme because they lack compassion. The truth is that under the surface of these rationalisations, there are still sad, angry and anxious feelings but they are suppressed. It is these suppressed emotions that are the main cause of physical kundalini symptoms - especially the famous (or rather infamous) head pressure. Healing can only take place when we are honest with ourselves and acknowledge our weak, unenlightened and "negative" thoughts and feelings and develop love and compassion towards ourselves.

But there are also many people who think too negatively - they hate themselves or they screw themselves deeper into their suffering by blaming other people and the world around them too much. These people must learn to take responsibility for themselves and try to see the positive in difficult situations. One advantage of all our problems is, for example, that they can be used to develop on our spiritual path by allowing us to practise more patience, compassion, forgiveness or assertiveness.

Therefore, we should try to be more honest and compassionate if we have a tendency for rationalisations or we should try to think more constructively if we have a tendency towards self-pity and blame others too readily for our problems.

Calm abiding (samadhi) versus life energy

Unfortunately, in some spiritual schools, peace of mind and calm abiding are overemphasised and life energy, together with love and compassion, are neglected. I have had some clients who meditated too much on inner peace and ended up in extreme states of utter passivity, depression and even paralysis. One client, for example, was unable to get up from her meditation seat after several hours of calming down all internal mental activity. She mentally called for help until her meditation teacher appeared, talked to her and thus enabled her to free herself from her paralysis. Several other clients reported that through years of meditation on calm abiding they became increasingly depressed until eventually, they had to give up this meditation practice.

On the other hand, I also had clients who worked too intensively with their inner energies, for example through qigong, until their kundalini symptoms became very debilitating - most of all causing insomnia. They, too, had to give up these exercises eventually.

As always, we should try to avoid all extremes and find a middle ground between concentrating on peace of mind and working with the life energy by harmoniously connecting the two. For example, we can begin our meditation practice with ten minutes of calm abiding and then switch to more active forms of meditation such as visualisations, chanting or working with the energies in the chakras. Alternatively, we can start with some yoga postures and then go on to practise exercises that emphasise peace of mind. Ideally, however, we should always practise the concentration on life energy and peace of mind simultaneously, which means practising energetic exercises with a completely relaxed mind.

A healthy sense of self versus egolessness

As a group, my clients often feel too attracted to teachings about egolessness and neglect the development of their more psychological sense of a healthy self-confidence. Consequently, they often find it difficult to assert themselves adequately in interpersonal relationships or defend themselves against selfish people.

There are also whole spiritual schools such as (neo-)Advaita that over-emphasise egolessness (also called emptiness) and reject any preoccupation with the conventional ego, such as making an effort to build better self-confidence and healthy ego-boundaries. This one-sidedness can have, yet again, many negative consequences. For example, some people who teach these beliefs claim that ethical behaviour and belief in karma are superfluous since the ego is "just an illusion" anyway. They, therefore, neglect investigating themselves in order to behave kindly and root out egotistical behaviour. Unfortunately, their belief of having no ego results in *complete identification with their (denied) ego.* If this delusion goes far enough, they may completely ignore their conscience (or superego) and can become unscrupulous or even cruel to other people - the complete opposite of being a spiritual person. In the worst-case scenario, teachers of such doctrines become charlatans and ruthlessly exploit their students because, if these students also believe in egolessness, they will find it almost impossible difficult to defend themselves against domination by their teacher. For example, when a student tries to rebel against a tyrannical guru, the guru can simply accuse them of "acting out of ego" to force them back into submission. All of this may sound incredibly absurd but it is, unfortunately, a widespread dynamic.

For some of my clients, the teaching of egolessness also causes fears as they believe that enlightenment amounts to killing their sense of self. Tibetan Buddhism helps us to unite harmoniously the opposite pair of egolessness and a psychological sense of having healthy self-esteem through the doctrine of the two truths. This teaching says that we exist as infinite free space (which is the egolessness or emptiness) and *at the same time* the conventional (or relative) sense of self remains fully functioning so that we can behave conventionally and constructively. We can understand this doctrine more easily if we remember our physics lessons. As we have all learned, atoms consist almost exclusively of empty space in which only a few absolutely tiny "particles" of energy move around. And yet our foot hurts when we knock it against a stone. This means that the absolute level of emptiness in the atoms simultaneously co-exists with the things as they appear to us in an everyday way.

For our spiritual and personal development, this means that meditative experiences of our mind as infinite and luminous space can free us from the perception of our limited ego-self with all its worries, doubts and frustrations. These experiences of bliss open the way to ultimately unite with our deity without fear of being wiped out in the process. Nevertheless, we also have to take care of our conventional self, which may still find it difficult to cope with the expectations of our boss at work, our partner or with raising our children. These two strands of development – the spiritual and the psychological - run in parallel but can mutually benefit from each other. Experiences of blissful oneness in the meditation may shake us free to find new ways out of a relationship crisis. More conventional self-esteem, which we can develop through psychotherapeutic methods, will allow us to be more courageous in meditation and become more spiritually open.

Just as I have described in the previous sections, our goal should be to unite this pair of opposites into a harmonious whole and avoid any extremes of overemphasising one pole at the expense of the other.

Power versus love

The most fundamental and therefore the most important pair of opposites is power and love. As a group, my clients often emphasise love more than power and, therefore, easily become victims of narcissistic and dominating people. Many of my clients have problems fencing off from selfish people, partly because they find it difficult to understand the motivation of these people and partly because they wrongly believe that exercising their power is somehow "sinful" or otherwise incompatible with their spiritual path.

In the relationship with themselves, many of my clients also have a reluctance to take powerful action against their disturbing symptoms. I have already discussed this problem in the section about control versus surrender. Too many clients allow their symptoms to flood themselves without trying to control them. Also, they often adhere to spiritual teachings that say that one should "simply observe" disturbing feelings. Unfortunately, this approach offers little help in the turbulent kundalini process and can even make things worse. What we observe and give our attention to becomes energised and stronger - just like pain becomes more prominent when we fully concentrate on it.

There are many phrases my clients use that show that they give power to others instead of taking the reins of their lives confidently into their own hands. They say, for example, "I don't know what I am supposed to do with my life" as if there is someone else who has the power to tell them what their purpose is. Or they might say, "it's (not) meant to be", "the universe wants me to" or "why doesn't God help me?" All these expressions indicate a belief that there is an outside power that determines or should determine what happens in their lives.

The rejection of power is just as problematic in the kundalini process as the rejection of love. It leads us to feel overwhelmed by our symptoms, by other people or by paranormal experiences. It also stops us determining

94

our path in life by handing over power to vague, indefinite "authorities" that we do not even really know. Therefore, it is very important that we stop giving away our power and that we value its development as much as we value the development of love.

My advice is to deal with selfish people and with our own disturbing symptoms like a loving parent deals with their children - with love but also with a bit of strictness - so that the children know that they are loved but that they cannot dominate their parents. All the exercises in this book are aimed at establishing this important balance between love and power.

In my counselling practice, I less often see clients who overemphasise the development of power but it could express itself, for example, through the use of supernatural powers for ego-aggrandisement or for making money or, worse still, posing as a charlatan or even a cult leader. This development often occurs when the kundalini has been awakened in people with personality disorders who still identify with their lower, animalistic impulses and who have neither empathy nor a proper conscience. Unfortunately, I personally know quite a few such people and also regularly hear from my clients about those kinds of charlatans.

Love versus power is the most important of all pairs of opposites because the perfect balance of the strongest power and highest love represents the highest potential of a person. Power without love is pure selfishness and love without power is useless because it cannot be used to influence the world for the better. The perfect union of love and power, however, leads to "powerful love" or "loving power", which can be used to exert the strongest and simultaneously most loving influence in ourselves and other beings. If we use these two forces in complete harmony and at the same time to the highest extent, we will realise what is called enlightenment or the union with God.

Chapter four
Higher-consciousness healing

In this chapter, I will introduce higher-consciousness healing and in the later chapters I will show how to apply it to different problems. This method is a transpersonal psychotherapeutic healing modality that I developed 20 years ago and that has brought successful healing to thousands of people. Transpersonal means that in higher-consciousness healing we connect the psychological and spiritual aspects of a person. I have described this method in detail in my book *Higher-Consciousness Healing* but here I will explain this method again including a few short-cuts and a few extra points to apply it to kundalini problems. I would also like to assure you that this technique has never made any kundalini problems worse but only calms down all symptoms in the fastest way and then dissolves them completely.

Higher-consciousness healing is based on Tibetan Buddhist methods and differs from traditional teachings firstly through the fact that it is a compressed combination of different meditation techniques and, secondly, that I have used my knowledge as a psychotherapist to apply this technique specifically to psychological problems and kundalini symptoms. The method is therefore not a dubious New Age exercise and it can be practised with the confidence that many variations of similar meditations have been used with great success for millennia by Buddhist practitioners around the world.

Traditional psychotherapy is of only of limited use for kundalini problems because a client in a spiritual awakening process hungers for spiritual answers and solutions. Unfortunately, if someone asks traditional spiritual teachers for guidance with their kundalini symptoms, they will often find little help for the many psychological aspects of the kundalini syndrome. It is only through the integration of spirituality and psychology that I was able to help over a thousand clients in the fastest way to rid themselves of their unpleasant kundalini symptoms and then enjoy the awakening process more positively.

Arousal and calming of the kundalini

To understand why higher-consciousness healing helps so well with kundalini symptoms, we need to understand what arouses the kundalini and what calms it down. Since this process is fundamentally a process of expansion of consciousness, it is therefore fuelled by all mind-expanding techniques such as mindfulness exercises, Vipassana meditation, reincarnation therapy, psychoanalysis and all other methods and activities that make us more aware in one way or another - like reading spiritual books and attending seminars for self-development. Furthermore, the kundalini gets aroused by all energy work such as yoga, tai chi or qigong or any treatment by energy healers because these exercises and treatments melt "the ice" in our energy body and bring up new material from our subconscious to the surface. Furthermore, all emotionally intense experiences will fuel the kundalini because strong emotions often result in even stronger emotions. A fourth way to fuel kundalini is to adopt a general attitude of wholeheartedly surrendering to everything and refusing to control anything.

People who have difficulties with their kundalini process and suffer from many symptoms need to reduce or even stop all spiritual and mind-expanding techniques for a while, including reading spiritual books. The same applies to all meditative physical exercises, breathing exercises and energy treatments such as reiki, acupuncture or homeopathy. It is also important to reduce all intense emotional experiences, for example by avoiding relationship dramas as much as possible and anything else that could upset us. Intense emotions also include experiences of ecstasy and bliss and if someone finds it hard to cope with their symptoms of awakening, they should reduce such experiences until they feel a bit better. They should also check whether they believe that they "have to" surrender to all their experiences and understand that this attitude will only intensify all their symptoms.

To calm the kundalini energy, we should first of all understand that we can influence it and, to a certain extent control it, if we know the right methods. Of course, one of these methods is higher-consciousness healing, which I will explain below. The quintessence of higher-

97

consciousness healing is love and deep relaxation and it is exactly these qualities that will act as a balm to all our out-of-control kundalini symptoms. Therefore, we should reduce all mind-expanding methods and, instead, practice higher-consciousness healing. We should also support this work through grounding activities such as walking, gardening, swimming or cooking.

It is important to understand this see-saw of consciousness expansion at one end and love with relaxation at the other end and then rebalance these factors to make the kundalini process flow steadily without over-heating it. When our process calms down too much, we can refuel it again through mind-expanding methods, strong emotional experiences and a lot of devotion. But when too much difficult material from our subconscious or the paranormal world appears, we can soothe and heal ourselves with higher-consciousness healing.

The practice of higher-consciousness healing

Higher-consciousness healing is a technique that requires practice and will produce a gradual improvement, just as we need to practise a musical instrument to get better step-by-step. In other words, when we use higher-consciousness healing daily, we will gradually feel better but sometimes we may experience days when we are a bit worse. We should not be alarmed by these little ups and downs but always keep practising diligently as if we are learning a new language, a musical instrument or a physical skill like skiing.

There is no such thing as a "bad practice day" or a "bad meditation". Every practice day and every meditation is *always* a success because it forms the basis for further improvements. It is therefore important that we practise in a relaxed manner and kind of "play around" with these exercises like a child instead of trying very hard to force things, only to tense up again. We should also avoid comparing today`s meditation with previous peak experiences because such experiences happen - just as their name indicates - only very rarely.

Higher-consciousness healing teaches us to control our energy body (or emotional body) and, over time, we will be able to turn our emotions and accompanying physical symptoms on or off with the same ease by which we control our physical body. This might sound amazing but it is just as easy (or difficult) as learning to ride a bike or learning to swim.

Unlike many other spiritual techniques, higher-consciousness healing will not produce further kundalini arousal and has been proven over many years in thousands of sessions with kundalini clients to be extremely safe and free of side effects. There is no danger in overusing this method, either. On the contrary, the more you practise it, the more you will benefit from it. You can practise, for example, one or two formal sessions of 10 to 30 minutes each day and the rest of the day you can playfully use this method "on the side" while doing all sorts of other activities.

You do not need to be able to visualise well when using this method; it is enough if you can somehow "imagine" things just as children do when playing. If you find that hard too, you can create simple drawings on a piece of paper. If you find it difficult to concentrate, you can talk out loud to yourself and tell yourself each part of the exercise or ask someone to read it out to you or make a recording of it. You should always imagine yourself from inside out rather than looking at your body from outside.

Sometimes my clients worry that they are "just imagining things" during this exercise and, therefore, that it will not be effective. But this is not the case at all and one should simply proceed playfully and not worry if everything is just fantasy or reality. The healing effect will soon be tangible and that is surely not imaginary.

Some parts of the visualisation require strong concentration where you have to change the inner images that appear in your mind. Do not give up on doing this and keep trying until you succeed in imagining the images the way *you* want to imagine them. Remember, you are the boss in your energy system and you can and need to bring it in order - just like a parent needs to assert certain rules of behaviour in the family in a gentle but clear way.

Exercise: Higher-consciousness healing
First step: Your higher consciousness

Think of *your higher consciousness. This is the being with the highest wisdom and love in the whole universe. It's like a father or mother being who loves you from the bottom of their heart. Name your higher-consciousness by the name that suits you best (God, Goddess, Heavenly Mother, Divine Father, Jesus, Buddha, etc.) Imagine this being enveloped in beautiful light in your heart in the centre of your chest. You can also imagine this being like a ball of light but please do not forget that your higher consciousness is a living being and not something material like a lamp.*

The light of *your divine father or mother now radiates into your entire body which you imagine as hollow and begins to caress you gently and lovingly - comforting you from the inside. It caresses you especially where you feel physical or emotional discomfort. The light also radiates around you as if your higher consciousness lovingly hugs you. Imagine your higher consciousness telling you all the things that you would have liked to hear from an ideal mother or father when you were a child.*

Second step: The protective bubble

Imagine *the light of your higher consciousness expanding into a ball of light around you that is as big as your outstretched arms. The bubble has a solid outer border that is about ten centimetres or four inches thick.*

Go along *the border of your bubble with your inner eye and check if it has any holes, cracks or other imperfections. Don`t try too hard doing this, be playful. You can also try to touch the wall with your hands to check for any holes.*

If you *find any problems with the boundary of your protective ball, imagine a magic substance and repair those holes. If the ball is too narrow or is collapsing, imagine an inner steel framework that supports the ball from inside as if it was a three-dimensional umbrella. If the ball floats uncomfortably above the ground, fix it onto a concrete base in your mind. If the ball flies away, tie it down with big ropes. If any other problem crops up, just invent a solution and imagine implementing it.*

Every time you imagine the bubble, try to imagine it being completely perfect until you succeed. Do not give up on this.

This bubble *is your inner sanctuary. See if you feel safer now when you feel enveloped by it. If this is not the case, thicken the outer walls of your ball. If you feel as if hostile people or creatures attack your bubble from outside then imagine a second ball that surrounds the first ball at a distance of several metres. Your "enemies" stay outside the second ball and you barely notice them now.*

Third step: Self-love

Tune into *the love of your higher consciousness and love yourself as if you were your own best friend hugging you. Sincerely and kindly say to yourself, "I wish myself to be happy and healed."*

Check if *you have any resistance to this love, such as a feeling of being undeserving of this love. If this is the case, say to yourself, "I love myself with all my problems and weaknesses and especially with (insert your resistance here)." For example, if you think, "I'm not worthy of being loved because I have too many negative feelings," then say to yourself, "I love myself with all my problems and weaknesses and especially with all my negative feelings." Imagine yourself like a suffering child who you want to help.*

If you *still find loving yourself difficult, think of someone you can easily love. This can also be an animal. Wish this creature to be happy and to be healed. If you can feel a loving feeling, quickly turn it onto yourself without changing it. Try to look at yourself with the same compassionate love as you would look at a small suffering child or animal.*

Imagine *that all your problems are solved and you are really happy now.*

Fourth step: Sending love to other people

If another *person is involved in your problem (perhaps because they have hurt you, because you grieve for someone or because you have harmed someone yourself), imagine that person in a second ball of light. This bubble sits between the hands of a second emanation of your very large higher consciousness. Push your higher consciousness with the* other person in the ball so far away from yourself that it feels the most comfortable.

Imagine that light starts to flow between the hands of your higher consciousness and fills up the person in the ball from the bottom up. The light will bring healing to this person. If the person has done something bad to you, the divine light will bring them to their senses and helps them to see themselves as they really are. (There will be more about this part of the exercise in the fifth chapter.)

Fifth step: Work with the energy body

Check where in your body you still feel any negative symptoms in the form of painful emotions or physical pain.

Think of your body as hollow and the negative symptom as a contraction of energy. This cramping is symbolised by a tight flower bud.

Smile lovingly into the spot of tension.

As you exhale, imagine the flower bud opening and the contraction of energy dissolving. Imagine that your higher consciousness stands in front of you and you can trustingly open yourself to him or her. Relax the spot of tension as much as possible.

These five steps of higher-consciousness healing are the foundation for the alleviation of all kundalini symptoms. In the following sections, I have provided a few additional pieces of information for each of the steps.

First step: The higher consciousness

Nowadays, many people follow spiritual teachings that more or less say: just stay in the here-and-now, let go of your ego and all your problems will be solved. Or even: you do not need to do anything because you are already enlightened!

While this advice contains a grain of truth, it is also very misleading. It is tantamount to telling a child who wants to be a ballet dancer, "just stand on your toes, lift your legs extremely high in a graceful manner, keep the perfect balance and you are a prima ballerina." As you can see, this advice is theoretically correct but will not be of much practical use for the child.

In the same way, some spiritual teachings stoke the illusion that spiritual progress is extremely simple when, in reality, it requires a lot of work and practice. To make progress towards enlightenment, there is so much more to do than relaxing in the here-and-now. In particular, letting go of the ego is not easy at all because the ego works like a kind of addiction within us to either dominate others or to pity ourselves as a poor victim. According to Buddhism, all our suffering stems from this "attachment to our ego" and this also applies to all our kundalini symptoms.

The first and extremely important step in freeing ourselves from our ego attachment, and therefore also from our kundalini symptoms, is to build a devoted relationship with our higher consciousness. For this reason, we begin the healing process by making contact with our higher consciousness. Everyone can imagine their own higher consciousness in exactly the way they desire: as God, as a goddess, like a light being, like Jesus or the Buddha, etc.

We should always keep in mind that our higher consciousness is a being and not something material or abstract, such as "the universe", "energy" or "the ground" or something similar. Instead, we should imagine our higher consciousness as a father or mother being with whom we can begin a trusting relationship as if we are their child. This child-parent relationship is extremely comforting and immediately helps us to feel a bit better and more protected. It also counteracts the pride of our ego, which is eager to see itself as completely "independent" and "not needy" - neither of which is true. For the same reason, it is also necessary to see the higher consciousness always as another being and never as an idealised form of our own "higher self". If we think of our higher consciousness as our higher self, we will probably include our limitations in this image, which would defeat the purpose of the exercise.

We should always imagine our higher consciousness as the being with the greatest love and wisdom in the universe and not be content with "spirit guides" - as is customary in spiritualism - or with New Age angels. No, whenever we open ourselves up to a higher being, we should go to the highest level possible because only then can we be sure that we will receive the very highest help. It does not matter if we think of an enlightened person who once lived, such as Jesus or Anandamayi Ma or a heavenly being like the Christian God or Prajnaparamita - the "Great Mother" of all the Buddhas.

In my experience, most people in the kundalini process find it relatively easy to get in touch with their own higher consciousness. But if you still have doubts about the existence of the divine and wonder if this is all just an illusion, you should visualise (or sense) your higher consciousness as a kind of "healing image" and only be interested in whether or not the image is helping you and do not need to concern yourself with the question of God's existence.

The higher consciousness, as we work with him or her in this exercise, is a mother or father being and not like the Christian concept of God who created the world and directs our lives. Such a directing God is illogical because, if he existed, he would save the good people from suffering, which is obviously not the case. Those who believe in such a guiding creator God often get angry when they realise that despite all their piousness, they have to endure just as much suffering as other (not so good) people. In the fifth chapter, I will explain in more detail how to let go of such anger at God. For the moment, let us explore the understanding that our higher consciousness is like a loving parent who very much wishes us to be happy but - just like real parents – cannot do our homework for us. This means that our "heavenly parents" can give us love and emotional support but they cannot solve our problems for us. Receiving this love and consolation is an important first step in overcoming all our kundalini symptoms.

To receive love from our divine father or mother, we imagine that this being resides in our heart in the middle of our chest, fills us with light and love and caresses and hugs us initially from within and then from the outside. The caressing should especially be done at the places in our body where we feel pain or negative emotions.

We can also imagine that our divine mother or father says exactly the kind of things we would have liked to have heard from our biological parents when we were a child. It is also very beneficial to think that our higher consciousness is our true father or our true mother who will accompany us through all our incarnations while our biological parents always change and are less important. This idea alone will replace hundreds of therapy sessions in which we may talk about our childhood wounds and yet cannot find a true solution for those injuries. But higher-consciousness healing offers us a solution through the experience of having infinitely loving parents so that we can heal all our childhood deficits in a deeply satisfying and long-term way.

Some people worry that it may not be possible to have their divine parent all to themselves because they imagine that their heavenly mother has to take care of many other "children" as well. This is especially the case when someone thinks of known divine figures like Jesus or White Tara. We can solve this problem by understanding that our higher power can occur in an infinite number of emanations and therefore each person can have their very personal divine father or mother all to themselves.

In very rare cases, some people experience pain when they imagine that their higher consciousness is in their heart. If this happens, they should imagine that their higher power is in their stomach behind the belly button and let the light radiate from this place.

Second step: The bubble

When we imagine the bubble of light around us, its boundary must be strong and intact. This boundary is semi-permeable - it lets in good and loving vibrations and blocks off everything negative. It symbolises our healthy ego boundaries and if it has holes, cracks or dents, it is a sign that we have difficulties fencing off from people and easily become dominated by others.

In my work in many thousands of therapy sessions, I have always found that holes and cracks in our bubble can be healed relatively easily by imagining a magic substance repairing them. Once we have done this, our fears diminish almost instantly, we feel safer and can assert ourselves in conflicts more easily. There are no limits to our imagination when it comes to repairing the ball around us and we can picture everything that will help us to make our bubble whole and strong again. We can, for example, screw on a steel cap, "brick up" the holes, "pour in cement" or whatever else comes to our mind. If the ball flies off, we can tie it down with steel chains and if the lower part is missing, we can put the whole bubble onto a concrete base and then "pour in cement" at the bottom or repair the lower area in any other way we can imagine.

If we feel that the ball around us gets attacked by beings from the outside, we can imagine a second sphere around us that is significantly larger than the inner bubble and thus protects us more effectively against all attackers. If our bubble feels too small and tight, we can unfold a kind of steel frame inside it like a three-dimensional umbrella that creates enough space for us to feel comfortable in our refuge.

Holes in the bubble almost always occur with people who have either been mistreated or have taken drugs. If you have not taken any drugs, holes are often an indication that family members have dominated you or still do. If you want to, you can try to mentally look through those holes to see who has made them. In many cases, you will quickly receive an intuitive answer to this question. In the fifth chapter, I will describe how to deal skilfully with such domineering or abusive people from your past and present.

If you find a hole over your head, it often means that you do not want to be in this world and that you would rather like to escape into heavenly realms. This often leads to physical weakness, many ailments, difficulties to be "rooted" in life and to assert yourself against other people. In such a case, you should make it clear to yourself that you are in this world to work on your karma and that it would make more sense to tackle this task with all your heart instead of trying to escape it. Then you should close the hole above yourself - just like all other holes in the bubble and remember that your higher consciousness already resides within your own heart and that you do not have to look for him or her "up there" in the sky.

A hole at the bottom of the ball could mean that something has "pulled the rug from under your feet" or that you do not feel you are "on safe ground". You should close this hole as described above and you will probably be amazed just how much safer you feel just by doing this.

Some people do not feel comfortable with the concept of a bubble around them and would rather not have one at all. In such cases, I point out that it would not be wise to leave all one's doors and windows open at night and, likewise, it is not wise to go through the world completely unprotected psychologically. Sometimes, I also show my clients pictures of Tibetan Buddhist deities who are always surrounded by a ball of energy. If even the Buddhas need their bubbles, surely we need them as well!

At this point, the question may arise as to why we should have healthy ego boundaries when the ego is supposedly only an illusion anyway and that, according to Tibetan Buddhism, the attachment to the ego is the cause of all our problems. The answer is that we can only transcend our ego when it is relatively healthy. In other words, we cannot become enlightened if we feel anxious or depressed most of the time. The "leap" into enlightenment (or at least into higher spiritual states) can only succeed when we have positive self-esteem and loving, healthy relationships.

Also, according to Tibetan Buddhism, enlightenment does not happen from one day to the next (as it is sometimes falsely claimed) but one can expect many years in which one has more and more frequent and longer "enlightenment experiences" that, over time, increasingly consolidate and ultimately become one's main state of mind. During this phase, the person falls back over and over again into their old and limited self-awareness. The healthier, happier and the abler they are to have loving relationships, the easier it will be for them to stabilise their mind in the state of enlightenment. In Tibetan Buddhism, this process is sometimes described as milk (enlightenment) that slowly drips into water (our old ego) and thereby transforms the water into milk over a long period.

If you can imagine a bubble of light with firm boundaries around you without any difficulty then this is a good sign that your ego boundaries are in good condition. You will rarely feel dominated by other people, you have good self-confidence and you will rarely dominate others.

Third step: Self-love

Self-love is not only a feeling but mostly an intention for ourselves to be happy and healed. Therefore, loving ourselves does not mean that we find ourselves "great" but that we see ourselves, with all our problems and weaknesses, as we really are and then wish ourselves to be healed from all these issues. Self-love is more about self-compassion than self-admiration. We should avoid the latter because it can easily degenerate into narcissism. Compassion for ourselves is also different from self-pity, which is often mixed up with frustration and envy of other people. Some people are even angry at God for not helping them as they see fit. Self-pity is also often saturated with entitled attitudes such as the assumption that we have the "right" to be happy all the time. By comparison, self-love is a form of compassionate acceptance of all our problems and the kind wish that we can free ourselves from them.

Many people have problems with self-love, especially if they had an overly strict upbringing or are members of a guilt-inflicting religion such as Catholicism. But love and compassion do not need to be earned by good behaviour or some achievement but it is there even for the biggest "sinners". If you find it difficult to love yourself, you can imagine a little child that has similar problems to you and send this child your love by wishing for him or her to be happy and healed. As soon as you feel warm, loving feelings, you turn them onto yourself with the thought that you are not so different from this little suffering child. In this way, you can "outwit" yourself a little and, by repeatedly using this method, you can slowly become used to being loved.

Some people worry when they do not have a real *feeling* of love. But this is not a problem because higher-consciousness healing will work whether we feel very intense feelings or not. Love in this process is an intention and not just a feeling. If we have a truly loving wish for ourselves, it will affect our healing whether we feel very much love or very little. A beautiful feeling of love is more like sunshine - it comes and it goes - and we should not get frustrated or anxious if the sun does not always shine.

Some of my clients seem to me like orphans who have never experienced someone loving them. They are suspicious of the concept of love and are afraid that it will disappear very quickly. I explain to these clients that they should give themselves time to become used to being loved. Their mistrust will not disappear immediately, just as a newly adopted orphan cannot immediately trust the love of their new parents. But after a few weeks or months of constant love, the orphan - and we ourselves - will get used to being finally deeply loved and will enjoy this state as the new "normal".

Fourth step: Sending love to others

It is of the utmost importance for the healing of all our kundalini symptoms that we rid ourselves of all our old grudges. Many of my kundalini clients have had distressing experiences of abuse, neglect and trauma. To free ourselves from post-traumatic stress, it is often recommended to simply forgive our adversaries. I don't think that this is so simple. On the contrary, I believe that you cannot and should not simply forgive people who have mistreated a small child. It is not in our power to simply wipe away this guilt and trying to do so often results in a prolongation of an exploitative relationship. I have had many clients who were stuck in such relationships and for that reason suffered from depression, self-doubt, anxiety and many psychosomatic problems. The expansion of consciousness in the kundalini process does not allow us to continue to sweep these problems under the rug "for peace sake" but will instead confront us with the full extent of our pain that is caused by dysfunctional relationships.

In higher-consciousness healing, it is completely unnecessary to relive a particular trauma to find healing. On the contrary, I advise against regression techniques as they can lead to re-traumatisation. Instead, I recommend visualising the person who has harmed us within an energy ball between the hands of a very large higher consciousness and stating clearly and succinctly what this person has done wrong. After that, we simply decide to end our grudge against them, which is easier than most people think. It is like laying down our weapons. This approach is very different from forgiveness because we leave the guilt with the person to whom it belongs and we do not make any excuses for them. After we have

109

stopped grudging the other person, we wish for them to be healed and send them divine light so that they can see themselves as they really are.

We work in this way to liberate ourselves from our anger, which could otherwise harm ourselves psychologically and physically. This step does not at all mean that we condone the behaviour of the other person or simply forget it or otherwise just wipe it away.

In my experience, this process of saying the three sentences and sending love leads to complete and long-term healing of all the symptoms caused by negative relationships and trauma. I have worked with many hundreds of clients in this way (and with myself, too) and have seen over and over again that people have been able to completely free themselves from all post-traumatic stress. This technique also works when we are angry at a whole organisation such as the health system or the corporate world which destroys our environment.

We can work in a similar way with all the guilt we have accumulated when we have harmed other people, such as through having affairs. If we send light and love to the people who we have harmed, it will help us to raise ourselves to a higher level of consciousness from where we could never again commit such acts. I will give more detailed explanations on this topic in later chapters.

Fifth step: The work with the energy body

Working with the first three or four stages of higher-consciousness healing will alleviate and, in some cases, even eliminate our kundalini symptoms. If our problem does not involve other people, we can skip the fourth step and move directly on to the fifth step in which we work directly with our energy body.

During all energy work, we should always think of our body as hollow and look or sense where in our body we feel our negative emotions and physical symptoms. Once we have found this area in our body, we should make it clear to ourselves that all our difficult symptoms are simply a contraction of energy. We then proceed by visualising this contraction as a tight flower bud. While breathing out, we smile into the flower bud (our

110

problem area) and imagine that it opens up into a beautiful flower and thereby diffuses and dissolves all our negative feelings and other symptoms. While doing this, we can imagine that our higher consciousness stands or sits in front of us and trustingly open ourselves towards him or her. It is important to work in this way because all our tensions were created through our belief that "out there" is a hostile and frightening world that we need to close off from. But if we imagine that our loving, divine mother or father is standing in front of us, we do not have to close off anymore and can let go of our inner tension together with our pain.

There are a few different versions of the fifth step depending on our different negative emotions (anxiety, anger or depression) and I will describe in the fifth chapter how to proceed in each case. To work with physical pain, we need to add an extra short step, which I will describe in chapter six.

Very rarely it can happen that our symptoms are getting worse during energy work. We call this problem an energy over-load. If this happens, we give the overloaded chakra as little attention as possible. Instead, we simply relax this chakra and focus on the navel chakra instead. If the affected chakra is the heart, we can visualise our higher consciousness in the navel instead of the chest area.

How to practice once all your major symptoms have been resolved

Once you have resolved all major symptoms in the kundalini process, it is best to work with the first three steps of higher-consciousness healing as described and then prophylactically with all the chakras. We do this by smiling into each chakra with love and imagine that a flower bud in the chakra opens up into a beautiful flower towards our higher consciousness. We always start with the upper chakras and work last with the abdominal chakra. I have described general chakra work in more detail in my books *Enlightenment Through the Path of Kundalini* and *Spiritual Joy*. By proceeding in this way, we prevent new negative symptoms from arising and we increasingly unite with our higher consciousness.

In summary, I would like to repeat that virtually all my clients with many hundreds of different negative kundalini symptoms have been able to reduce their problems dramatically or eliminate them completely by applying higher-consciousness healing. Incidentally, this also applies to symptoms that were not triggered by the kundalini process. This method works with ordinary psychological and psychosomatic symptoms just as well.

Those who regularly practice higher-consciousness healing can gradually learn to contract it more and more until you can finally practice it in almost one single instant. One does this by putting oneself in a higher "vibration" of divine love, relax all inner emotional tensions, meet all beings with compassionate love and preserve clear boundaries everywhere – all instantly and at the same time. Anyone who succeeds in stabilising this state has reached the highest human potential - enlightenment.

So, higher-consciousness healing is not just a small therapeutic exercise that you should practise only until you feel better but a practice that can bring your entire spiritual development to the highest fruition. Therefore, you should practise it every day until the end of your life. It is the quintessence of Tibetan Buddhism and I have the full support and blessing of my teacher Garchen Rinpoche, one of the lineage holders in the Drikung-Kagyu lineage, to teach this method as a Buddhist teacher.

Chapter five
Working with disturbing feelings

To resolve our kundalini symptoms, we should always start with our disturbing emotions and only try to heal our more physical symptoms in a second step. In many cases, just working with emotions resolves physical pains and energy blocks simultaneously. This works because all physical kundalini symptoms - without exception – consist of half-suppressed emotions. Many of my clients are surprised by this statement because energy symptoms and pain in the kundalini process do not usually feel like emotions at all. In the sixth chapter, I will show you how to recognise an emotion within a physical symptom and then dissolve this emotion - including the pain - with higher-consciousness healing. In this chapter, I will focus only on painful emotions and give detailed instructions for dissolving them with higher-consciousness healing. I introduced the first three steps of this method in the previous chapter and here I will explain in more detail the fourth and fifth steps to heal and dissolve anxiety, depression and anger.

Dissolving disturbing emotions is very simple once you correctly understand what they consist of and how to transform and dissolve their "substance". You may remember the ice-block metaphor from the first chapter: ice stands for numbness; painful physical symptoms are represented by half-thawed ice; our emotions are like water and when the water turns into steam, we experience our mind as bliss. In this metaphor, one can see that, in essence, physical pain, negative emotions and bliss are all made of the same substance or energy but that emotions and pain are contractions of this energy (ice and water) while bliss is the greatest relaxation (steam).

To dissolve negative emotions, the main principle is to transform and relax the substance of the emotion (water) in order to experience the "final product" of ecstasy (steam). To achieve this, we first have to "warm" the water and we do this on the psychological level in higher-consciousness healing by sending love to ourselves *including* all our painful feelings.

Secondly, we diffuse and disperse the energy cramped in the symptom by relaxing the exact place in our body where the negative emotion manifests. We do this by smiling lovingly into the body part and visualise a flower bud opening from this place towards our higher consciousness in front of us while we exhale. Through this approach, "the water transforms into steam" by diffusing and releasing it with each exhalation of breath. In summary, it is all about penetrating our negative emotions with love and deeply relaxing the body part in which they manifest and all painful feelings like anxiety and anger will simply disappear - it truly is as simple as that!

I have not invented this approach myself - it is based on the Tibetan Buddhist understanding of our minds and related meditations. My contribution is to tailor this spiritual approach to psychological and kundalini problems and to teach it in a way so that anyone can use it, no matter what spiritual background they have. I have used this method successfully in many thousands of hours of therapy with my clients and have regularly seen that it can free people from even decades of chronic anxiety, depression and other symptoms within a few days or weeks.

With higher-consciousness healing, there is no risk that emotions are just being suppressed because we dissolve them and transform our mind into a healthier state. In the twenty years that I have been working with this method, it has never, to my knowledge, produced any unwanted side effects or a renewed suppression of feelings.

It is important to recognise, however, that negative emotions do not necessarily disappear after a single intervention. They are, after all, just like water, which always tends to condense again even if we have dissolved some of it (evaporated it into steam). On the psychological level, this means that we all have quite persistent emotional patterns and need some perseverance to leave these patterns completely behind. We can compare this process to learning to play a musical instrument. It needs a practice phase before our body adjusts to the new movements and can perform them almost automatically. Similarly, the dissolution of negative emotions is a technique that we can practise and master with a bit of patience. There is no trick, no self-hypnosis and no placebo effect involved because it is not necessary to believe in this method. Higher-consciousness healing is a simple self-help technique that everyone can learn, practice and then master. In fact, the method is so simple that even many children have used it successfully. But we should not be deceived by the simplicity of higher-consciousness healing. We have in front of us the quintessence of Tibetan Buddhism as it was developed and diligently practised by male and female sages residing in monasteries and icy caves in the Himalayas for over a thousand years.

On our road to recovery, we should expect a few zigzags and should not despair if we have a bad day. When practising higher-consciousness healing, the adage is true, "practice makes perfect". We need to be persistent with this exercise and always immediately dissolve even the smallest negative emotions before they become huge and hard to manage. We can compare this process with gardening. If we always pluck out little weeds immediately, gardening will be easy and happen quite quickly. But if we wait until huge stinging nettles and brambles have developed, the process will be much more difficult.

As I mentioned earlier, we should deal with our disturbing feelings like a mother would parent her wild children - with love but also with a certain strictness. It is about understanding that we are the boss of our mind and determine which emotions we want to have and which we do not want to have. In the kundalini process, it will not be enough to just observe our wild emotions or just watch them go by as it is taught in many meditation classes for beginners. On the contrary, there is a danger that our feelings will even increase by observing them too intensely because everything grows that we give attention to. In the kundalini process, we need a stronger method to deal with our disturbing emotions and this method is higher-consciousness healing.

I also strongly advise against simply "letting out" emotions to get rid of them - for example by shouting, crying loudly or punching pillows. This will certainly not work because the more often we express our disturbing feelings, the more we strengthen those mental habits and the harder it will be to be healed from them. There is also the danger that our friends and family will become very annoyed with us if we simply act out our emotions towards them. The fact is that you cannot just "spit out" thoughts and emotions like water in order to get rid of them. The only true option for healing is to *transform* our emotions from ice into water and then into steam as I explained before.

If we practise this for long enough, we will ultimately be able to do it in a single moment and continuously remain in a state of bliss. I have described this ultimate approach in more detail in my book *Spiritual Joy*. It is called Mahamudra or Dzogchen in Tibetan Buddhism and is based on the understanding that our true nature is bliss, which is simply covered up by "veils" of confusion and ignorance. By removing these veils, you return to your true nature that was always there.

The energy patterns of emotions

All emotions take place in our energy or emotional body, which penetrates our physical body and protrudes slightly beyond the body's boundaries. For this reason, we can experience our emotions sometimes slightly in front, next to or above our body. But most often we feel our feelings within the energy centres in our body - the chakras. In Tibetan Buddhism, these chakras are located in the top half of the head, throat, chest, solar plexus and just below the belly button.

Each person has a unique pattern in which chakra they experience their emotions but there are also general patterns that I typically observe in my clients. For example, most people experience sadness in their heart or eyes, anxiety in their solar plexus, chest or throat and anger in their jaw or abdomen. For those who have not consciously explored these patterns in themselves, you can close their eyes and imagine the three basic emotions - fear, sadness and anger - one after the other and check in which part of your body the feelings manifest.

Just like water, our emotions also have directions in which they flow. In depression, the energy flows downwards. In fear, the energy contracts and pulls back. When we feel aggressive, the energy moves forward like in a punch or it will burn within us like a flame if we restrain our anger. With joy and love, our energy rises and spreads up and out.

116

To resolve depression, we must therefore reverse the downward flow of energy so that it can rise. We should concentrate on joyful thoughts in this process because the antidote to depression is joy. To dissolve anxiety and all fears, we must relax the contraction of energy and spread it out. This relaxation or peace is the antidote to all fears and anxieties. And to let go of anger, we need to replace the forward-moving energy with loving wishes towards the person we are angry with and penetrate the restrained anger that is burning within us like flames with kindness and relaxation because this is the antidote to all anger. I will explain in more detail how to work with all these emotions in the individual sections about the different emotions. For now, I just want to reassure you that it is not difficult – even children can do this.

The better we can perceive these emotional energy patterns in our body, the easier the process to dissolve them will be. Although this process of dissolution is very simple in principle, we should also prepare ourselves for new and more subtle emotions appearing in the kundalini process and acknowledge that the process of purifying our energy body will, more or less, carry on for the rest of our lives. This process is our spiritual path and it can be a great joy to commit to it. You can compare it to liberating a beautiful old painting that was hidden under many layers of old paints.

Anxiety and fears

By the term "anxiety" we understand all feelings of nervousness, fear, panic, phobias etc. Anxiety can cause many physical symptoms such as dizziness, the feeling of leaving the body, chest pain, heart palpitations, weakness in the legs, humming in the head and many others. All of these symptoms should gradually reduce through the exercise below.

We begin by asking ourselves what we are afraid of and try to take all practical steps to alleviate these fears. This is, of course, a very general piece of advice but some people are so confused in the kundalini process that they disregard it. However, many of my kundalini clients do not have specific fears but experience more generalised anxiety or free-floating fears. With the following exercise, you can reduce all specific and free-floating forms of anxiety and, with a little bit of perseverance, you will also be able to eliminate them. Remember, it is not necessary to visualise well when doing higher-consciousness healing. Simply feeling, sensing or somehow knowing is enough.

Anti-anxiety exercise

Start with the first three steps of higher-consciousness healing as described in the fourth chapter. Watch how the bubble around you creates a sense of security.

Find the place in your body where your feeling of anxiety manifests, e.g. in the solar plexus, heart or neck. Imagine your sense of fear as a tight flower bud.

As you exhale, imagine the flower bud opening up and a beautiful light flowing out of it in small waves, spreading out towards the ends of the universe. Always breathe through your nose. Imagine your higher consciousness standing in front of you and open trustingly towards him or her.

Once you have completely exhaled, your lungs will be empty. Stay with empty lungs and do not inhale as long as you can but without making any effort. Count the seconds of how long the light spreads while you refrain from breathing in.

Before you get uncomfortable, breathe into your lower belly again. Put one hand on your lower abdomen and feel how your stomach slightly expands against your hand as you inhale. Do not hold your breath after breathing in but immediately breathe out again while imagining the flower bud opening up again. Again, count the seconds as the light travels towards the ends of the universe before your next inhalation.

Breathe in and out relatively quickly. Your chest should not lift visibly when you inhale, only your lower abdomen should move. Do not extend your breaths in any way but breathe naturally. Do not breathe deeply but allow your breath to become quite shallow. When inhaling, do not imagine that the flower is closing - nothing happens during inhalation.

Breathe in a constant rhythm: relatively quickly in and out, then have a long break with empty lungs. Try to extend this break slowly. If you can hold your breath with empty lungs for 10 to 15 seconds, you are on the

---

> *right track.*
>
> **When the** *feeling of fear or anxiety moves to different parts of the body, follow it mentally and imagine a flower bud opening in all these places - one after the other - until you have dissolved the fear everywhere.*
>
> **If you** *find the breathing part of this exercise difficult and you are tensing up, try doing the exercise without the conscious breath.*
>
> **When** *the anxiety has lowered to a tolerable level, smile gently into the place in your body where you can still feel it. Your smile will speed up the residual dissolution of anxiety.*
>
> **If you** *like, you can combine the exercise with a simple stretching exercise. For example, when you exhale, you lean forward or sideward.*

The anti-anxiety breathing technique aims to reduce the volume of air that flows into your body. For some people, this sounds like a bad idea because they believe that more air is better. But over-breathing is just as harmful as over-eating. If we do it once, it does not do too much damage but, over the long term, it is quite detrimental. I did not invent this advice myself. The same advice is given by ordinary doctors to people who have panic attacks. As it is well known, they should breathe into a paper bag which throttles the supply of oxygen to their lungs. When we practise the breathing part of higher-consciousness healing, we try to achieve the same effect but without the use of a paper bag.

The fear-reducing effect of this exercise is explained in the following way: when we are anxious, we breathe in too much air and, in this way, overload our blood with oxygen. But the body needs time for the oxygen to move from the blood to the organs and muscle tissue. This process happens in the break after exhaling and thus, paradoxically, we get more oxygen the longer the break between the exhalation and inhalation lasts. In contrast, during anxious hyperventilating, the oxygen simply remains in the blood while the body is actually suffocating. This dynamic adds a physiological fear of death to our psychological anxiety, which, of course, only exacerbates our distress.

All forms of meditation automatically slow down our breathing in the way I have described in the exercise above. Sometimes the breath seems to come almost to a complete standstill. We do not need to be afraid of that because this process is extremely healthy as it will provide us with more life-giving oxygen than before. Oxygen is our elixir of youth and this is one of the reasons that people who have meditated for many years often look younger than their peers.

People who are prone to a lot of anxiety should try to slow down their breathing all day long. It only takes a few days or some weeks until the slower breathing becomes automatic and will reduce many fears almost all by itself. You cannot get any side effects with this method; it is just very calming. Anyone who is so frightened that they cannot concentrate on this exercise should simply read it out to themselves - just like to a frightened child.

People who are afraid of specific things should gradually expose themselves to the frightening situation (exposure therapy). They should begin by mentally imagining the scary situation while practising the anti-anxiety technique. If they can handle that well, they should expose themselves to the problematic situation in the smallest steps possible while continuing to practise this method. As I explained earlier, we should deal with our feelings as we deal with children and not allow the children (our fears) to dominate us. We are the "boss" - not our fear!

Depression and sadness

The work with depression and sadness refers to all forms of sadness, hopelessness, despair or depression. We can also add anhedonic depression, which is a condition in which we cannot feel positive emotions.

We start by trying to identify where in our body the feelings of sadness and depression manifest, e.g. in our head or chest. We then imagine that there is a mouth in this part of the body that says something that expresses our depressed feelings, for example, "it's all too hard", "no one loves me" or similar things. When we notice irrational statements, we should correct them, such as, "many things are hard but not everything" or "no, my son loves me". If we have a lot of negative thoughts, we should write this thought correction down and read it daily until we know them by heart. We can also combine the anti-depression exercise below with the

120

gratefulness exercise as described in chapter five.

It is also quite possible that we encounter deep-seated grudges when working with depression, such as, "my mother treated me badly" or something similar. If we feel such a grudge, we should also work with the anti-anger method described in the next section in addition to the anti-depression exercise.

Anti-depression exercise

Start *with the first three steps of higher-consciousness healing as described in the fourth chapter. Focus especially on the love that your higher awareness gives to you and the love you give to yourself. Love yourself* **with** *your depression - just as you would love a sad little child.*

If you *find it difficult to love yourself because you condemn yourself (e.g. "I don't love myself because I don't deserve it"), then say to yourself, "I love myself* **especially with** *my feeling of being undeserving" or "I love myself* **especially with** *my feeling of being unlovable". No matter what you think is bad and unlovable about yourself, always put a layer of loving balm on top of it so that nothing in you remains unloved. If you find the word "love" difficult, you can say, "I am compassionate with myself even though... (insert here what you think is unlovable)."*

When a *feeling of love and compassion spreads within you, you will feel a little feeling of peace or even a sense of well-being. As soon as you feel this feeling, smile gently. You can also just think of a beautiful memory that enables you to smile a little.*

Now imagine *a beam of energy surges up from your abdomen in the middle of your body and "explodes" in your brain like a fountain or a firework rocket. Imagine this with momentum, seeing the energy shooting up in a single moment from the bottom to the top.*

When this *energy "explodes" in your head, smile and try to think happy thoughts. You can, for example, think of a happy memory or imagine how a dream will come true.*

If you *feel a slight sense of joy, concentrate on it. Observe it and relax. Try not to grasp at this feeling and do not try to make it somehow better or bigger. Just watch it and you will notice how it expands all by itself.*

> **Repeat** the energy surge to your head from time to time and try to stay in a positive state of mind as long as you can. As soon as you feel positive emotions, watch them and feel them spreading out within you.

Once you have learnt to create a positive feeling through this exercise, you should then keep focusing on it in daily life throughout all hours of the day. You can do this, for example, while doing housework, on your way to work or whenever you do not have to concentrate on other important things.

The biggest obstacle to success with the anti-depression exercise is the thought that "it cannot be that easy to get out of depression". But it really is so easy and I have had many clients who have freed themselves from years of severe clinical depression in this way.

Crying spells

For many people, an occasional crying spell is a cleansing and relaxing experience. For some people, however, it degenerates into frequent and never-ending periods of intense sobbing, which they would rather not experience. If you would like to shorten such crying spells, I have an easy solution for you. It consists of sitting up with a very straight spine, keeping the head upright, keeping the eyes wide open and your hands away from the face. In this posture, you can allow the tears to keep running and within three to five minutes you will find that they will stop all by themselves. This super simple "exercise" works one hundred per cent.

Suicidal tendencies

First of all, I would like to state that anyone who has acute suicidal tendencies should go immediately to a doctor or an emergency department and access professional help.

People who only occasionally play with the idea of suicide should reflect on what they believe will come after such a death. Tibetan Buddhism teaches us that all our mental tendencies persist after our death and will be greatly enlarged. So, if someone dies in a depressed and despairing state, they will be even more depressed and desperate afterwards. All world religions agree that it will only make everything worse in the afterlife if someone commits suicide. If you are open to these teachings, suicide is not a solution.

Besides, there is the problem that spiritual and psychotherapeutic practices do not work very well as long as one keeps the option of suicide open as a back door. If people have this attitude, they do not work with the necessary willpower and determination that is necessary to change their life for the better. It is indispensable that suicide is not seen as an option because only then will it be possible to overcome depression and despair.

Grieving the loss of our loved ones

We all suffer when we lose someone we love. This will be the case even if we are already well advanced spiritually. There is a little Zen story that illustrates this fact: A student saw his teacher crying loudly and asked what had happened. The teacher said, through his sobs, that his son had died. The student was confused and asked, "But did you not teach us that all suffering just comes from our attachments? Why are you crying like that? "The teacher simply replied," My attachment to my son was very great." The following exercise will help us ease our grief in the event of the loss of a loved one.

Exercise: Dealing with the grief for a loved one

Start *with the first three steps of higher-consciousness healing as described in the fourth chapter.*

Focus especially on the love that your higher awareness gives to you and the love you give to yourself. Love yourself **with** *your grief - just as you would love a sad little child.*

Imagine *the person you have lost is in a second ball of light in front of you. This ball of light sits between the hands of your very large higher power.*

Talk to *this person and tell them everything that is on your mind. "Listen" with your intuition for their answers.*

Imagine *divine light between the hands of the higher power starting to*

---

flow and filling the person's body in the ball. Imagine that this person now becomes one with the divine and is overjoyed.

Repeat *this exercise as often as you feel the desire to contact the deceased person.*

Anger and resentment

When working with anger, we should, first of all, realise that anger - just like fear – also has a healthy function. It is a warning sign, for example, that we are being exploited or manipulated in a relationship. We should not try to "meditate away" this form of anger but, instead, use it to try to change our relationship or distance ourselves. I will say more about difficult relationships in chapter eight. The exercise below is only for out-of-control anger and useless long-term irritation or grudges, which are feelings that can harm our mental and physical health.

I have many clients who believe that, from a spiritual point of view, all forms of anger are "wrong" and spiritually advanced people never have these feelings, let alone express them. But Tibetan Buddhism teaches us something different. Here we can find the so-called wrathful deities who act with power and a certain aggression against anything that impedes the spiritual path. There are, for example, images that show a bloodstained female goddess dancing on a male corpse. The dead body is a symbol of the worldly ego, which must "die" before we can wake up to our divine self.

There are also Buddhist teachings saying that a small amount of anger is beneficial because it makes people more intelligent. You can see things a bit more clearly with a bit of anger and you will recognise more easily what is right and wrong. School teachers or judges, for example, will do their job better if they are not the kind of person who always finds everyone just nice and has no opinion about anything. From a psychological perspective too, the suppression of anger can be extremely damaging and can cause depression, chronic fatigue, pain and even psychosomatic auto-immune diseases.

On the other hand, there is a teaching in Tibetan Buddhism that says that a single moment of rage will wipe out a large number of good deeds.

The accuracy of this teaching is easily seen when we consider that a single tantrum can break apart a long-standing friendship. Therefore, our task is to find the middle path between the extremes of self-justified aggression and complete submission. This task can never be easy and the following guidelines should help us find this middle ground.

What to do if you are angry?

Avoid all strong expressions of anger like shouting at other people, hitting pillows or screaming alone in the car. These activities create negative karma when other people are being attacked and if you express your anger alone, you will only reinforce your habitual anger.

Ask yourself, if the conflict is worth a fight. What will be the long-term consequences if you now tell the other person your frank and angry opinion? Be aware that you have the freedom to choose your battles.

Think about whether you want to use the provocation as an opportunity to practise patience and tolerance.

Consider whether you are willing to accept the provocation as your bad karma. Be aware that this would cleanse your bad karma.

Think about whether humour may be the best response to certain provocations. Especially in the family, humour can dissolve much aggravation and anger towards our partner and children.

Be aware that it is perfectly normal and harmless to have aggressive thoughts about other people from time to time. Such thoughts alone do not trigger bad karma; only actual words or deeds will. However, chronic anger or resentment are harmful to our mental health and our physical health since they weaken our immune system.

If you want to take action against your "enemy", I suggest strongly that you practise the anti-anger exercise below for a few days before you do it. Always resist the temptation to disparage or dominate the other person or take revenge. Only try to protect yourself and make it clear to the other person that they have done something wrong. If necessary, hand over the case to the police or other authorities.

The following exercise is designed to help you to rid yourself of all your old and unnecessary resentments. You can also use it to mentally prepare for conflict discussions. This exercise is *not* meant, however, to replace these discussions or avoid all conflicts. In chapter eight, I will describe in more detail how we can transform relationships in which we often become angry and upset. The exercise will also help anyone who suffers from frequent feelings of impatience, boredom, frustration or annoyance because these are all signs of subliminal, smouldering anger. This exercise can also be used for anger at large groups of people, for example, the health system or our capitalist economy.

Anti-anger exercise

Start with the first three steps of higher-consciousness healing as described in the fourth chapter.

Focus especially on the love of your higher consciousness and the love for yourself. Say, "I love myself with my anger" and imagine comforting yourself.

If you do not know why you are angry, feel into your body to notice where you sense the anger and imagine a mouth in this body part. Let the mouth express the anger. For some people, maybe only swear words will come out. Try to sense who you would want to say those words to. In all likelihood, they are your family members or (ex-)partners.

Imagine the person you are angry with in front of you in a second bubble of light. This ball of light sits between the hands of your very large higher power – one hand is underneath the bubble and the other on top of it with fingers touching to surround the entire bubble. Move the higher consciousness with this ball away from you until the distance feels just right. You can even place your divine parent with the bubble on another planet.

Say three sentences to this person in the following way:

Firstly, explain briefly and clearly what this person has done wrong without any explanation or apologies (i.e. not, "he had a bad childhood" etc.)

Secondly, say, "I stop grudging you now." Make it clear to yourself that chronic anger is harming you physically and psychologically and that you

---

want to let it go. This does not mean condoning the other person's bad deeds or somehow discounting or forgetting them.

***Thirdly,** say to the other person, "I wish you to be healed". Imagine how divine light starts flowing between the hands of your higher power filling the body of the person in the bubble from the bottom up. When the light reaches the brain of this person, they can see themselves as they really are and, thereby, recognise all their incorrect intentions and actions. If possible, intuitively perceive how this person responds to these insights.*

***If you** wish a complete separation from this person, let them disappear in their ball over the horizon.*

***If you** still feel some anger in your body, smile into that part of the body and penetrate it with kindness and love. Simultaneously, deeply relax this part of your body by imagining a flower bud opening and light radiating out of it.*

***Now** do everything that is necessary to clarify the conflict with the other person. If it is a very old conflict where there is nothing left to discuss, you can just forget it.*

Anger at God

Quite a number of my clients are angry at God. Usually, this happens because they believe that God has withheld help from them or has somehow abandoned them. To let go of such anger, we should first of all understand that this anger is based on a kind of childlike religious faith. If there was a God who helps good people, our world would be in a much better situation than it is. Secondly, we should make it clear to ourselves that God has not abandoned us but that we have turned away from him. This is clearly visible through the anger we feel towards him.

To let go of our anger towards God, we use the above exercise and imagine God in the second ball of light (but without a large higher consciousness holding the bubble). We say to him, "I'm sorry that I expected from you what you cannot give anyone. I wish you to be happy and healed." Then we see God filled with divine light smiling at us lovingly.

Many of my clients respond with astonishment and a little bit of fear at this suggestion. But I can assure everyone that this practice will quickly

127

resolve all anger at God. We will also become better at taking responsibility for ourselves and thus create the basis for a happier life.

Noise and other sensitivities of our senses

Many people in the kundalini process suffer from a pronounced sensitivity towards noise. The disturbing noises can come from neighbouring apartments, dogs barking, engines and especially all the sounds that people make to enjoy themselves, such as loud music, etc. Most of my clients report that they do not like living in a noisy city any longer but rather prefer living quietly somewhere in the countryside. In addition to suffering from disturbing noises, many people also suffer from increasing self-doubt and see themselves as "over"-sensitive or even "neurotic" and find it hard to accept themselves with their sensitivity.

Noise-sensitivity is basically an anger problem because we have an aversion against the "intrusion of noise into our energy field". Some people experience this aversion so strongly as if they feel physically attacked. They may say things like, "the constant music drives me insane" or, "his slurping is so unbearable that I could kill him".

As a first intervention with all over-sensitivities we should try to focus more on our navel chakra. This focus will generally stabilise us, so that we are less like a flag in the wind that reacts immediately and strongly to all outer influences. We can practice this concentration easily when we are walking and during all other forms of exercise. In daily life and during all meditations, we should also feel repeatedly into our abdomen and anchor our consciousness in this place.

Obviously, we should also take all practical steps to reduce all excessive noise in our environment. For example, we can teach our children to play more quietly and if people around us behave in anti-social ways, we should complain where necessary. As usual, we should precede these practical actions by sending love to the noisy people before confronting them. If our entire environment is too noisy, we should also consider moving or changing our job.

If we did everything on a practical level to reduce our noise problem, we can use higher-consciousness healing and use it in the same way as we use it for all other things that make us angry as explained in the anti-anger exercise. As always, we start with the first three steps as described in chapter four. In the third step, we should give a lot of love to ourselves and say to ourselves, "I love myself *with* my sensitivity and annoyance" and inwardly comfort ourselves like we would comfort an irritable baby. We should also make it clear to ourselves that our sensitivity has been caused by our kundalini process. So, we are not necessarily neurotic but we are more like many other mystics in world history who retreated into hermitages to have enough quiet for their meditations. In the fourth step, we pay close attention to where in our body we tense up when we are confronted with annoying noises. We smile lovingly into these body parts and try to relax them by using the image of the opening flower bud that I explained earlier. While we are practising, we should avoid flooding ourselves with noises that stress us.

We can apply this meditation to all our other sensitivities, as well. We focus generally more on our navel chakra and use in parallel the higher-consciousness healing method. We should just not forget that it will be impossible to return to our old, numb self that appeared more robust. We will never regain this numbness, which is actually very good because our sensitivity is also a kind of higher intelligence that we can use to do much good. It is the beginning of clairvoyance and we should take good care of our developing psychic abilities by adapting our life as much as possible so that our senses are not constantly over-stimulated.

Anger and frustration after experiences of bliss

Sooner or later in the kundalini process, we will experience prolonged states of bliss and ecstasy that are so beautiful and intense that it is almost impossible to describe them in words. It may sound surprising but bliss and ecstasy can cause much anger once they are over. In a way, they are not unlike drug highs from which you may become very irritable and suffer with a hangover afterwards. As beautiful bliss and ecstasy are, they confront us with a significant challenge to integrate them into our lives. Anger and frustration after experiences of bliss happens for three main reasons:

Experiences of bliss always open our unconscious mind: ecstasy melts the ice faster in our subconscious mind, which we have talked about in our ice-block metaphor and thus allows our suppressed rage to surface. We should be prepared for such difficult emotions when we experience great bliss and work with this anger as described in the exercise above.

The world seems more annoying after experiences of bliss: Our world with its many problems can appear as even more frustrating when we experience it against the backdrop of perfect bliss. It is like a black dot that looks even blacker on a white background than on a grey one. This frustration teaches us that it is necessary to be patient and accept that the path to complete enlightenment is still very long. It is also important to withdraw from irritating triggers and arrange our life, as much as possible, so that we do not experience unnecessary aggravation. We should also always practise the anti-anger exercise until it becomes second nature.

If it has become easy for us to experience ecstasies, it is important to channel this bliss into helping other beings. For many people, this wish will come naturally and it is important to try to find some form of platform to put the wish into action. It is also important to try to cultivate bliss feelings in all the chakras and not just in a single chakra. We start with the upper chakras and, finally, we should mainly work with the navel chakra. The focus on the navel is important because the happiness in the navel chakra is more stable and easier to integrate into normal life instead of alienating us against our environment as bliss in the higher chakras sometimes does. More information about how to work with bliss and the chakras can be found in my books *Enlightenment through the Path of Kundalini* and *Spiritual Joy*.

Ecstasies can cause megalomania: the biggest problem with experiences of bliss is that they can provoke megalomania in people who have a tendency in that direction. If this megalomania is not recognised as such but the person identifies with it, narcissistic rage can easily occur when other people "dare" to criticise them or do not submit to their exaggerated entitlements. Instead of saying, "I *feel* wonderful feelings of happiness" a person with this problem thinks, "I *am* wonderful. I am now enlightened and all beings must show me respect" or, "I *am* blissful, pure and good. I cannot do anything wrong because I am perfect" and then they start to lie and to dominate other people.

To counteract the risk of megalomania, it is of great importance to integrate the worship of a divine being into our spiritual practice and, ideally, to have a spiritual teacher in human form who we consult with regularly. Without the knowledge that there is someone above us to whom we are accountable, there is a very real risk that our ego may become so intoxicated by these extraordinary experiences of bliss that we lose our moral bearings.

To prevent megalomania, we should always watch our ego or self-image as our ecstasy begins to rise and strictly reject all megalomaniac ideas about ourselves. Instead, we should observe the qualities of ecstasy and notice that it has no core, no boundaries and no substance. Although it feels like our true self, it is "nothing at all". This "nothing" is called emptiness in Buddhism and it is crucial that we use experiences of bliss to dissolve our limited ego identity rather than building a megalomaniac sense of self. I have described this process in greater detail in my book *Spiritual Joy*.

In summary, if you receive feedback from your environment that you have recently become a bit more selfish and arrogant, you should rigorously try to control those tendencies and, if necessary, work more closely with a spiritual teacher. The relationship with a partner can also be a great source of help and I will describe in the eighth chapter how to use your partnership or marriage as a hotbed for spiritual growth. In extreme cases, it is necessary to forego meditating on joy altogether and, instead, focus solely on developing more love and compassion.

Raw animalistic aggression

Some people are shocked to find strong, animal-like aggression in themselves that is full of hatred, envy and sadistic joy. The shock is even greater for people who believe that all bad behaviour stems from being wounded and that real evil does not exist. Unfortunately, they will experience a rude awakening from this naïve view when they find exactly these horrible impulses within themselves, especially if they cannot find

131

the slightest wound that they could make responsible for them.

In the best-case scenario, we can transform these nasty impulses into humour but we have to be quite skilful at doing this. Otherwise, we should try to accept these experiences as humbling for our ego and therefore beneficial for our spiritual path. We should then proceed to practise the anti-anger exercise and send our "victims" plenty of love.

Traumatic memories

For many people in the kundalini process, memories of traumas from this life - or perhaps even from a previous life - come up. Usually, these are memories of painful experiences connected to parents, ex-partners or bullying at school. In all of these cases, people can proceed with the anti-anger exercise as described before. This will be helpful even if they do not feel any acute anger but just dull resignation and sadness.

Many people who are victims of abuse tend to blame themselves for their experiences. They say, for example, that they "have caused the sexual abuse themselves", that it is their "own bad karma that caused the abuse", or even that "they should not play the victim card since there are no victims". Unfortunately, these uncompassionate views only lead to even more suffering. Someone who was mistreated or sexually abused as a child is very much a victim and the concept of karma does not change that at all. People who had such awful experiences should try to free themselves from all guilt-inflicting concepts and, instead, use higher-consciousness healing to receive comfort from their higher power and give a lot of love to themselves.

After they have done the anti-anger meditation a number of times, they should ask themselves whether they want to take action against the people who abused them. This is an important option that we should not disregard, especially when it comes to sexual abuse and other criminal acts. They are, however, in no way forced to report people. It is just an option that they should be aware of.

For less serious mistreatments, they can ask themselves whether they want to confront the other person to get an apology. If this is not an option, they should distance themselves from this person. It can never be healthy to relate to someone who has abused them and pretend that nothing ever happened.

"Strange memories"

Some people experience "memories" during the kundalini process that do not feel completely like real memories. They are often very frightening yet they do not seem to have the realism of "genuine" memories. This often refers to childhood sexual abuse where my clients are not completely sure whether it really happened or not.

Through the detailed work with my clients, I have seen a number of times that this can happen when a person remembers a fear of a sexual assault but that nothing actually took place. It happens, for example, quite often that a grown man has sexual feelings for a little girl but never acts on his feelings and always behaves correctly. Ordinarily, the girl will not notice anything and neither will she have "strange memories" once she has grown up. Through the expanded consciousness in the kundalini process, however, she may remember that "something sexual" was "there" but yet without any "real" memories. Such experiences can lead to much confusion and anxiety.

I have worked with a number of clients through such "strange memories" and they always concluded that they were remembering the *fear* of sexual abuse and not an actual abuse itself. I have, of course, also worked with many victims of actual sexual abuse. For these people, there was never any uncertainty as to whether the abuse had happened or not.

In either case, the real abuse or the remembered fear of abuse, one should use higher-consciousness healing as described in the anti-anger exercise. This is best done with the help of a compassionate therapist. If the person also experiences strong fears, they should also work with the anti-anxiety breathing.

Traumatic memories from past lives

It is very rare for my clients to have spontaneous memories from previous lives. I never encourage clients to access these memories - as it is done in reincarnation therapy - because, in my experience, it could re-traumatise them. It is also unnecessary to remember past lives to solve our current problems because there are just endless chains of memories of past lives in which the roles of perpetrators and victim-identities alternate so often until the whole picture becomes somewhat irrelevant.

The truth is that all our problems can only be solved in the now and higher-consciousness healing will help us to achieve this in the fastest and easiest way. The following exercise is for people who experience spontaneous memories of traumatic past lives and it will help them to deal with these memories constructively:

Exercise: Dealing with traumatic memories of past lives
Start with the first three steps of higher-consciousness healing as explained in the fourth chapter.
Imagine going to yourself in a former life and tell yourself how beautiful your life has now become and how much freedom they will have in a later incarnation. Comfort the person as best as you can and tell them that everything will turn out well. For example, if you remember yourself in a previous life as being incarcerated in a prison, mentally go into that prison and comfort yourself.
Imagine the other person from your memory in a ball of light sitting between the hands of your higher power. Imagine how divine light starts to flow between the hands of your higher power filling the body of the person in the bubble and thereby completely comforting them.
Repeat this exercise every time you have unpleasant memories from previous lives.

Guilt feelings

In the course of the kundalini process, many people experience guilt feelings now and then. This happens because we are motivated in this process to make our lives healthier and more loving and, therefore, our readiness to have a bad conscience increases. For this reason, our expansion of consciousness also encompasses all our wrongdoings which will come unpleasantly into our mind sooner or later. There is a tendency in traditional psychotherapy to quickly wipe away all such guilt feelings and

134

only focus on the woundedness of the client. But it will not help a client if we simply say, "just forgive yourself." On the other hand, many traditional religions focus too much on guilt and Catholicism does this most strongly with its concept of original sin. This has left many people with deep wounds of unhealthy shame that can be difficult to heal. When working with guilt, we must distinguish whether we are dealing with genuine guilt where we have actually harmed other people or if we are dealing with unwarranted guilt feelings that stem from inferiority complexes or religious teachings that were unnecessarily harsh or misunderstood.

Unjustified guilt feelings are based on a lack of self-worth but, unfortunately, many people find it difficult to distinguish actual guilt from inferiority complexes. As a basic rule, we have only accumulated real guilt if we have actually harmed other people. Violent thoughts or a strong desire to take revenge alone do not create bad karma. For this reason, we can quickly dissolve unnecessary guilt with the first three steps of higher-consciousness healing.

Some clients also feel excessive guilt for things they did as children or young teenagers. In these cases, too, I advise them to dissolve all guilt feeling with the first three steps of higher-consciousness healing. It is a scientific fact that the frontal lobes of the brain that enable us to have a bad conscience only really start to function in adolescence. This means that we are simply not able to make wise moral decisions as children due to biological reasons. If someone lied a lot as a child, stole money or did risky sexual things, this often points to neglect by the parents. This should then be clearly stated and dealt with through the four steps of higher-consciousness healing as described in the anti-anger exercise.

I have, however, also had many clients who harmed other people, especially through having affairs or neglecting their children. Surprisingly, many people do not understand why having affairs causes bad karma and sometimes even believe that they are the victim in such a scenario. These people often suffer from confusion, head pressure or other strange kundalini symptoms that they do not understand. This happens because their unconscious mind is well aware of their guilt but they suppress this knowledge. If these people can accept that they have hurt other people

135

and consciously repent these acts, their symptoms often improve.

Some of my clients have also done many other unpleasant things. In many cases, they wanted me to give them a method to rid themselves of their guilt and shame - just like you can liberate yourself from anxiety or depression with higher-consciousness healing. Unfortunately, this is not possible. If a person harmed someone, they cannot simply "wipe away" this guilt through therapy or spiritual exercises. In my opinion, they should not even try because the pain of their bad conscience is precisely the protection that will prevent them from doing these things again. My advice in these situations is to make shame a friend who will lead us on the right path. The following exercise will speed up this process:

Exercise: Dealing with genuine feelings of guilt

Start with the first three steps of higher-consciousness healing as described in chapter four. Imagine that your higher consciousness loves you because they believe that you can improve. In the third step (self-love) say to yourself, "I am compassionate with myself even though I ... (say here, what you did wrong)".

Imagine the person who you have harmed is in a bubble of light. Say to this person, "I am very sorry for what I did to you. I will do everything I can to make up for my behaviour. I promise never to do these things again. I wish you to be happy." Imagine filling the other person with divine light and imagine how that person becomes happy and smiles.

In real life, try to apologise to this person and make amends. If this is not possible or appropriate, consider how you can do something good in general. For example, if you have mistreated an animal, you could help out with an animal welfare centre or at least make a generous donation.

Continue to send love to the person you have harmed every day until you feel a lessening of your guilt-feelings. Depending of what you did, this process could take very long but that is okay.

Try to see your feelings of shame and guilt as your friends who will help you to stay on the right path.

It is helpful in this process to read books or reports of people who underwent a profound spiritual conversion. There is, for example, in Tibetan Buddhism, the famous story of Milarepa who, in his youth, killed many people with black magic but later reached enlightenment. There is a great book about Milarepa's life story by Evans-Wentz, a cartoon by Eva Van Dam and even a movie that you can watch on YouTube.

Chapter six
Working with physical symptoms

As I have explained several times before, there are no true physical symptoms in the kundalini process, only appearances that feel physical even though they actually take place only in the energy body. In other words, all physical symptoms are emotions that are half-suppressed, which means that we feel their pain but not yet their psychological content. I repeat, kundalini is not a disease and can never cause physical disease symptoms.

As a group, my clients enjoy very good health. It is rare for my clients to tell me about any illnesses and I almost never hear of serious afflictions like cancer or heart disease even though I work with many older clients. I attribute this to the fact that in the kundalini process, the desire to make our lives healthier in all respects bears fruit and, therefore, even my older clients are usually in good physical shape due to their healthy diet, a lot of exercise in nature and a generally healthy lifestyle.

It must be stressed, however, that it is quite normal for all human beings to become sick now and then even if they are in the kundalini process. Kundalini does not automatically protect us from all illnesses unless, of course, you have achieved the supernatural ability of spiritual healing. In this case, you can heal yourself and others simply with mental power.

When working with physical symptoms in the kundalini process, the aim is to make the half-suppressed emotions (that are stuck in the pain) conscious and then dissolve them with higher-consciousness healing in the usual way. It is therefore advisable to only start with this work, once we have already successfully alleviated all the emotions that we had in the first place. Most people will find that their physical symptoms already improve through the work on their emotions. On the other hand, if we start too early to work with our physical symptoms, then there is a danger to flood and overtax ourselves through too much emerging fear, sadness and anger.

Pain in the body

The distinction between kundalini symptoms and symptoms of real diseases is not always straightforward as the former can mimic real clinical ailments. For example, I myself once had all the symptoms of gallbladder disease but an ultrasound showed that my gallbladder was in excellent condition. It is, therefore, always advisable to go to a doctor first and take all the necessary tests to exclude real illnesses. As soon as you get the green light from your health professional, you can start with the following exercise:

Exercise: Dealing with physical pain

Feel your *pain and rate it on a scale from 1 to 10.*

Ask yourself: *If this pain was an emotion, would it most resemble fear, anger or sadness? Try these three emotions on like a glove and see if any of them fit. Name the emotion that fits best.*

Now imagine *your pain as that emotion and imagine a mouth in the middle of the pain/emotion and let the emotion say something. If you feel angry, start with, "I'm angry/frustrated/annoyed ..." and finish the sentence intuitively with the words that come to your mind. Try to say as much as possible without censoring your words. You may say completely irrational and childish things but consider it a positive thing that these words are now coming to light and are no longer suppressed within the physical pain. If you feel fear or sadness, start with, "I'm scared ..." or "I'm sad ...".*

Ask yourself *to whom would you want to say these things (maybe to an ex-spouse or a parent, for example). Allow your intuition to simply let someone appear without judging immediately. If nobody comes into your mind, that is okay, too.*

Now use *higher-consciousness healing as described in the fifth chapter to heal your particular emotion and the people who are involved in it.*

Check on *your scale to see whether your pain has already decreased a bit.*

Smile into *the place of your pain with deep love and imagine a flower bud opening within it, radiating divine light. Imagine your higher con-*

---

sciousness in front of you so that you can trustfully open towards him or her.

__If the pain__ is very persistent, touch it with your hand and perform a circular or rubbing massage on it. Press as lightly or as strongly as feels good. After a few seconds of massage, gently guide the hand away from your body with the radiating light in the direction of your higher consciousness. Repeat the massage as often as necessary.

__If the pain__ moves to another part of your body, follow it, smile into the new place as well and open the flower bud there as before. A wandering pain is a good sign because it shows that the problem is no longer "stuck" but has started to loosen.

When working with kundalini pain, we often have to be a little bit more patient compared to working only with emotions. The reason is that physical pain indicates that our inner conflict is more deeply buried in our subconscious mind than is the case with pure feelings. So, we should be prepared to work longer with these symptoms daily for days, weeks and sometimes even months and try to be patient and positively appreciate even small improvements.

Here is a case study to demonstrate how to work with physical symptoms: Michael is a 33-year-old accountant and suffered from strong pains in his shoulders that made it impossible for him to exercise. He also suffered from erection problems. When Michael performed the exercise described above, he realised that the pain felt like anger and when he tried to give words to this feeling, only swear words came out. Michael had an extremely hot-tempered father and he never wanted to be like him. Therefore, he had repressed all his anger but had, unconsciously, gone way too far in this process. After doing the above exercise for a few weeks, Michael was able to jog two kilometres, which was a huge breakthrough for him. His impotence, which he had suffered from all his life, also went away within a few weeks.

When pain and negative emotions become worse while practising

In very rare cases, the pain or associated painful emotions can increase when we focus on it in the way described in the above exercise. I mentioned the problem of energy overload already in the fourth chapter. This most often happens with pain in and around the chest and sometimes also in the head. This can be a sign that we inadvertently tense up while we are practising. It can also be a sign that we generally overfocus on the higher chakras and have neglected the lower ones and in that way have become imbalanced. If focusing on a painful area in our body makes us consistently worse, we should avert all our attention from this area of our body and completely ignore it for a few days or even weeks until the tension dissolve on its own accord.

It is helpful in these cases to focus more on the navel chakra so that the superfluous energy of the cramped and overloaded chakra can flow down to the navel. In this process, we should not even think or talk about the painful body part. If the painful area is in our heart, we can imagine all our feelings of love in our eyes or the palms of our hands (as in blessing or caressing) and simultaneously focus on the navel more often.

Involuntary body movements - kriyas

Kriyas are involuntary body movements that often occur at the beginning of the kundalini process. They can be anything from trembling or twitching to elegant hand gestures or even full-body yoga postures. We can compare kriyas with normal involuntary movements such as yawning, a shudder when we are disgusted or eyes that open wide in fear. Kriyas are harmless and are simply a sign that your inner ice-block is beginning to melt. When you surrender to these movements, they often feel liberating and relaxing.

There are, however, two ways of getting problems from kriyas if you do not deal with them correctly. The first problem arises from trying to abuse these involuntary movements as a means of nurturing "spiritual pride". For example, I sometimes receive emails from people who want to show me their kriyas because they think they are ultra-interesting. (They really are not.) I have also read reports that some people "show off" their kriyas at spiritual events.

Buddhist and Hindu literature repeatedly warns us against the danger of becoming attached to appearances on our spiritual path and abusing them to build up one´s ego. Of course, this also applies to kriyas. For this reason, one should try not to display kriyas in public and never boast about them. They are not a great "spiritual achievement" and abusing them for egoistical purposes is more a sign that someone is not spiritually advanced at all.

The second danger is to surrender too much to your kriyas for a long period until they are completely out of control and almost impossible to stop. This development is very problematic because I have had clients who could not leave their home anymore because of their involuntary body movements and other clients who were thrown out of meditation groups or had beaten themselves black and blue.

It is therefore of great importance that we always keep control of our bodies and consciously decide when and where we allow these movements to take place. The ideal is to experience these physical movements only internally and to stay outwardly still and perfectly controlled. If the kriyas consist in movements of the arms, for example, one should try to visualise these movements internally but let the real arms lie quietly in one´s lap.

If you cannot control your kriyas very well, you should say to yourself, "I am the boss and I control my body." Then you should try to control your kriyas as much as possible with muscle tension. For example, if your head is thrown back, place your chin on your chest and control your head in this way. If your arms twitch too much, you can even sit on your hands for a while. It takes only a few days or a few weeks for most people to regain control of their out-of-control kriyas. Once you have regained control, you can afford to let them run wild every once in a while but only when you are alone and in a safe place where you cannot hurt yourself.

Chronic fatigue and exhaustion

Many people in the Kundalini process suffer from phases of fatigue and exhaustion. As always with physical problems, we should make sure that medically everything is in order. Once we know that we are physically healthy, we can work with fatigue with the same exercise that we use to dissolve physical pain. We begin by asking ourselves where in our body we feel the fatigue and then follow all the other steps of the method.

Most people who suffer from fatigue believe that they have somehow lost their energy and that they need new energy. But this idea is not correct. The tiredness comes from the suppression of their feelings - especially anger - and it is this constant effort that robs them of their energy. It is also this "not-wanting-to-know" what they feel that literally pulls a veil of fatigue through their brain. So, the solution is to get in touch with their real feelings as described in the exercise about dissolving physical pain and then dissolve these emotions with higher-consciousness healing. It is also important to constructively address all conflicts with other people who are involved in these emotions.

I had quite a few clients who could rid themselves of extreme fatigue within a few days or a few weeks through practising higher-consciousness healing. Here is an example: Bruno was so tired that he almost could not talk to me when he came to his first session. He could not work, of course, and spent most hours of the day in a kind of half-sleep. When we discussed his situation, Bruno told me that his girlfriend gave male clients "tantric massages" which sometimes also included masturbating them. We discussed how Bruno felt about this and whether he considered this work to be prostitution. Bruno claimed that he completely approved of his girlfriend's work and that it certainly was not prostitution. However, his attitude changed in the days after our session and he suddenly realised that his girlfriend's work hurt him deeply. Of course, this development triggered a relationship crisis but Bruno's fatigue was blown away after only three weeks.

Supportive measures for chronic fatigue

Sleep eight hours every night but not more. Set an alarm, if necessary. Too much sleep makes you even more tired during the day.

Stay in an upright position throughout the day and never lie down. Lying down produces alpha and theta waves in the brain, making you tired.

If you are tired during the day, sit down comfortably but always keep your spine and head upright.

Keep your eyes open all day - even while meditating. Closing your eyes also produces alpha and theta waves in the brain and makes you tired.

Be ready to address all conflicts that you have with other people.

When the fatigue starts to dissipate and you feel more irritation and anger, do the anti-anger exercise and try to deal with the conflicts in your life more constructively.

Head symptoms

Kundalini symptoms in the head often do not respond as readily to the procedure that I have outlined above as other physical symptoms do. The reason is that the lower part of our head (chin, neck, jaw, mouth, cheeks, ears, nose and eyes) acts as a representation of our entire body. For example, tensions in the jaw may represent anger in our abdomen, tensions between nose and mouth may point to fear in our solar plexus and pressure on the eyes may be a sign of unexpressed sadness in the heart.

We can imagine a small humanoid figure on our face with the abdomen in our chin, the stomach around our nose, the chest and shoulders at the height of our eyes, the throat at the place between our eyebrows and the head on our forehead. For this reason, only symptoms above the eyebrows should be treated as true head chakra problems. With all symptoms from the eyebrow down, we need to work on the part (or chakra) of our body that they represent in addition to the work on the head.

People who experience frequent symptoms in their neck and face are often out of touch with the places in their body where these emotions actually originate. For example, frequent headaches resulting from neck tensions are often caused by anger in the abdomen that people are unaware of.

We can find out about our unconscious emotions in our body by relaxing the body part that corresponds to our head symptom and visualise an opening flower bud within it as explained before. During this work, we need to pay close attention to the slightest sense of discomfort or aversion. Once we have found any signs of negative emotions, we can dissolve them

144

as described in the fifth chapter. Therefore, with symptoms in the bottom part of our head, we often need to work both on the symptom in the head area itself, as well as on the corresponding part in our lower body.

Head pressure

A notorious symptom in the kundalini process is head pressure, which is a true head symptom corresponding to the head chakra with its topic of how we think and view the world. This pressure can occur at various points in the head and is either from the inside out or, vice versa, from the outside to the inside. Unfortunately, this problem is not easy to treat as it results from excessive positive thinking.

One might assume that positive thinking is always positive but, unfortunately, this is not the case at all. The following examples illustrate why excessive positive thinking can have very negative consequences: One of my clients with a strong head pressure told me about her wonderful marriage and how easy it was for her to deal with all her husband's quirks. She was completely shocked when her husband suddenly filed for divorce. Another client with bad head pressure had lost millions of euros through ill-conceived business ventures. Nevertheless, he was still convinced that he had many more "wonderful" business ideas, which angered his wife and endangered their marriage. Yet another client with head pressure had a boyfriend who pressured her to take part in a polygamous relationship with him. She agreed because his arguments seemed to be "positive" but emotionally she could not cope with this arrangement at all. The most common "positive thinking" of people with head pressure is having too high an opinion of themselves along with a tendency for complacency and narcissism.

Of course, many narcissistic people in the world are not in the kundalini process and do not suffer from head pressure. But when the kundalini has awakened, the unfounded idealisation of oneself will have negative consequences - most of all, head pressure. To understand this dynamic, we need to remember that the kundalini process urges us to be more honest, authentic and spiritual. Our ego, on the other hand, wants to continue to spin its fantasies and stories so that we ourselves, our ideas and our families always look good. This clash of the drive for authenticity on the one hand and the desire to stay in our "positive" fantasy world on the other hand takes place in our head-chakra. The truth and the fantasies literally press against each other and create the unpleasant head pressure.

The work with head pressure is usually very slow and tedious because no one likes to exchange the idealised opinions they have of themselves with more self-critical and realistic attitudes. Therefore, head pressure usually disappears much more slowly compared to dissolving fears or other physical pains that we gladly let go off. To get rid of head pressure, we have to be prepared to be much more self-critical than before. In that context, it is interesting that among my clients, men tended to idealise themselves and women often saw their partners in a more positive light than would be justified.

Occasionally, I had clients who were ready for this (self-critical) work and were able to reduce their head pressure significantly or even completely dissolve it. In most cases, however, it took a long time – even years - and required many "admonishments". Unfortunately, many of my clients with head pressure broke off their therapy with me, even though I was extremely careful when questioning their overly positive ideas. This shows how difficult this problem is to deal with.

I advise people with head pressure to seek feedback from a trust-worthy person and become radically honest with themselves. They should try to criticise all their smug, narcissistic and dishonest thoughts and actively look for even more selfish views in their unconscious minds. Particularly women should also be willing to be more critical of their partners or other people around them. To find these egotistical ideas and anger, everybody should look mainly in their lower chakras and try to make these chakras "speak" as I explained in the section about dissolving physical pain. If they find critical, aggressive, misogynist or other ugly views, they should not be too horrified but rejoice that they can now correct these attitudes.

Problems around sleeping

In the kundalini process, many people experience temporary sleep disturbances, nightmares, and insomnia. In this section, I will point out some practical solutions for all these problems.

Insomnia

One of the biggest problems with sleep in the kundalini process is the difficulty of falling asleep or staying asleep. These difficulties are due to the fact that our expanded consciousness sometimes does not allow us to sink into the unconsciousness that is necessary to fall asleep. It is even possible that we consciously experience our dreams. To dream, we need an increase in theta waves and for most people, these slow theta waves cause them to fall asleep immediately. In the kundalini process, however, we can sometimes consciously experience these so-called hypnagogic states where we dream but are still awake. We can even learn to consciously experience the onset of delta waves, which is the moment when we fall into a deep sleep state. This transition manifests with a small fear at the heart. Some of my clients who felt this fear mistakenly assumed that they had a serious psychological problem, which they did not.

The following exercise helps to consciously induce sleep. The interesting thing about this exercise is that it has almost the same effect on the brain as proper sleep and, therefore, we need a lot less sleep when we practise it. It is important to remind ourselves from time to time of this fact as we practise it because, otherwise, we can easily get frustrated. Unfortunately, anger is the great wake-up call and will make it even harder to fall asleep. Someone prone to having sleep problems should do the following exercise every day, even in periods when falling asleep is easier.

Exercise: Sleep meditation
Lie down *in your favourite sleeping position and imagine that you are in the arms of your (very large) higher power. You are protected and loved like a baby.*
Tell yourself *that you do not need to "really" sleep as long as you do this*

---

sleep meditation.

Relax all *the tensions that you can feel in your body. Imagine that all these tensions become runny like mush and drip down into your bed.*

Imagine *that your whole brain, especially your forehead, becomes like mush. Also, release your lower jaw.*

Imagine *that all your thoughts and feelings are just tensions and let them melt away like mush along with your brain.*

Continue *to relax your body, brain and thoughts in this way. Do this in a dozy way, without making any big effort or visualising anything.*

At some *point, you will notice that dream images emerge from your unconscious mind. You will know when this happens because these dream images have a distinct difference from ordinary thoughts that is easy to recognise. If you notice these dream images, it is a good sign that you are approaching real sleep. Just continue your sleep meditation and remind yourself that you do not need to "really" sleep.*

If you are *just on the verge of falling asleep, you may feel a little fear in your heart. Rejoice that you have come this far and continue to let go of the fear by imagining it melting away like mush - just like all other tensions.*

The most *important thing to remember is that you do not really need to sleep when doing this meditation and that it is sufficient to simply practise it to wake up refreshed in the morning, even if you have done it for a long time.*

Nightmares

Through our increased sensitivity in the kundalini process, our dreams can also take on a much more intense and realistic quality. For that reason, some people are prone to thinking that their dreams are now prophetic or otherwise "more real" than normal dreams are. This can create a lot of fear especially when people have nightmares. Fortunately, both of these ideas are not true. For dreams, there is always the rule that "a dream is always just a dream", so there is nothing to be afraid of. Even ultra-realistic nightmares are just very uncomfortable but never dangerous.

The only exception to this rule is having an inspiring dream of a divine being or a high spiritual teacher. These positive dreams can be confidently taken at face value and we can allow ourselves to be comforted and inspired by them.

People who often suffer from nightmares can try to "order" their unconscious mind in a friendly way to produce only beautiful dreams before going to sleep. Since we have easier access to our subconscious mind in the kundalini process, this strategy is often successful. To make our unconscious mind cooperate, we should speak to it as we would to a child who needs protection from danger - with love but also with an authority that does not tolerate any contradiction.

Sleep paralysis

Some people in the kundalini process experience states of sleep paralysis in which their minds are awake but their bodies are still asleep and appear paralysed. As with other sleep problems, this symptom can be traced back to their expanded consciousness that is now awake where before it was unconscious.

Sleep paralysis can be uncomfortable or scary but is completely harmless. You can end it quite easily by focusing on just one finger or toe and try moving it. Then you can move the whole hand or the whole foot, followed by the whole arm or leg and already the sleep paralysis is over.

Problems when waking up

Almost all of my clients report that they often experience uncomfortable emotions in the first moment after waking up and, therefore, often have a bad start to the day. They also frequently think that this is a sign of profound psychological problems but, fortunately, this is rarely the case.

Our unpleasant feelings arise from our subconscious mind, which is particularly open when we first wake up – firstly, because of the kundalini process itself and, secondly, through dreaming at night. Additionally, our willpower is still weak due to our drowsiness and lying in bed such that we cannot defend ourselves well against this painful onslaught. These three factors explain why we are often flooded with unpleasant material from our unconscious in the early morning.

To lessen and even completely eliminate this problem, we should make a habit of saying a simple prayer in the first second of waking up. The easiest prayer is to simply call for our higher consciousness just as a child would call for their parents. The Dalai Lama recommends the following little prayer, "Today, I want to develop for the benefit of all beings and I want to use all the experiences of the day to uplift my mind to a higher level." This prayer is very effective because it uses the word "want". As soon as we use this word, our willpower literally gets switched on and, in that way, we are much better able to control and transform our negative states of mind.

You can also create your own little prayer or simply practise the part of higher-consciousness healing that you like best. The most important thing is to practise regularly when you wake up in order to make it a habit so that you can better deal with the inundation of your mind with unconscious material.

Strange energy symptoms

There is an infinite number of non-painful but strange energy symptoms that can be experienced during the long kundalini process. Here is a small selection that are particularly common:

Trembling
Jerking
Tickling on or under the skin or deep in the body
Feeling that body parts have increased or decreased in size
Energy moving like a washing machine in the body
Rising heat
Shooting energies through the body
Cold sensations in different parts of the body
Feeling of energy blockages or energy stagnation in different parts of the body
Feeling like a snake is creeping around in you
Feeling as if a belt constricts you
Feeling as if ants crawl around on your body

Tingling energies anywhere in the body
Sexual feelings anywhere in the body

If these energy symptoms trigger pain or unpleasant feelings, you should work with them as explained in the sections about physical pain and emotions. Otherwise, the basic rule applies that all these sensations – just like kriyas - are harmless and simply indicate that the "ice" in your energy body is melting and will probably bring up new psychological material from your unconscious mind. As long as you do not have pain or unpleasant emotions, you can confidently ignore these strange energy experiences and just continue to practise higher-consciousness healing.

However, I have had clients who had problems with this simple advice. These clients were often young men who found it particularly unpleasant that they experienced sexual feelings in different parts of their body where they felt "they did not belong". They also intensely disliked the sparkling "champagne" feelings, which most people would find pleasurable. In these cases, I could only advise them to be patient and try to become more flexible instead of insisting that they should feel as numb as they did before.

Chapter seven
Working with mental problems

There are many forms of disturbed thinking that can happen in the kundalini process. This occurs because already existing negative and neurotic thought patterns are reinforced — just like negative emotions — and thus become bigger issues than before. What makes matters worse is the fact that many people in this process explain their strange experiences from the perspective of their old frame of mind and often misinterpret them. For example, they may become afraid of being physically ill or going crazy. Furthermore, their minds may also develop completely new negative thought patterns and can even produce horror visions or paranormal experiences that can cause a lot of anxiety and confusion. Through the stress involved in the kundalini process itself, it can also happen that the entire way of thinking of a person becomes disturbed. For example, some people experience phases of being unable to concentrate well.

The first step in responding to all these thinking problems is the anti-anxiety exercise from the fifth chapter because most forms of confused thinking are caused by fear. As soon as we feel calmer, our panic-stricken and confused thoughts will calm down as well and we will also be able to concentrate better.

My second piece of advice is to strengthen rational and fact-based thinking. As a group, my clients tend to overvalue their intuition and devalue rational thinking. They may say things like, "these are all just concepts" or "it's the mind that creates all problems". Unfortunately, these generalisations are not at all helpful and I have already described this problem in the third chapter about the middle path. Of course, it is a fact that deep, mystical experiences go beyond rational thinking but to integrate these experiences into our life, we definitely need our rational mind. Therefore, we should not devalue rationality and we should try not to deal with all our kundalini phenomena purely through our intuition.

The general confusion about the kundalini process can hopefully be alleviated through reading this book. Furthermore, I would strongly recommend avoiding reading all the horror stories about the kundalini on the Internet and only read information by authors who have a sound qualification. The danger of becoming confused and even exploited by mentally ill or confused people, by quacks or even charlatans is not insignificant in the beginning stages of a kundalini awakening.

One should also be very careful about talking to clerics or doctors about these experiences because one can easily be labelled as mentally ill or possessed by "demons", which would only lead to additional problems. Even well-meaning friends and family members are not always the best people to talk to because they are often afraid and may urge people in the kundalini process to take psychiatric drugs or go into psychiatry.

Negative thought patterns

In the kundalini process, all our thought processes are intensified and it is much harder to ignore negative thought patterns as we may have done before our awakening. Therefore, in this process, we are forced to put our wrong thinking in order just like we are forced to bring every other part of our life in order. In this section, I will describe typical negative thought patterns and how to heal them most effectively.

Negative self-talk

Many people have a bad habit of talking to themselves in a degrading way, of constantly scolding themselves and even insulting themselves. This bad habit should be corrected as soon as possible. As a rule, we should always try to talk to ourselves just like we would talk to our best friend. Therefore, we should begin immediately to replace all our self-pitying or self-degrading thoughts with constructive thoughts.

It is important to understand that we do not try to just think positively but aim to think *constructively*. Positive thinking can be very irrational and can even bring more suffering. On the other hand, constructive thinking is based on facts and therefore has a truly healing effect on us. For example, if we suffer from life-threatening obesity, we should not say to ourselves,

"I have an ideal weight" (which would be a positive but irrational statement) but we should say, "I love myself *with my excess weight* (or whatever it is that disturbs you about yourself) and I wish myself to be happy and healed". While positive thinking can lead to even greater denial and ego-delusions, constructive thinking remains on the ground of reality and is, therefore, a great help for positive change.

People who find it difficult to stop the self-insults simply by making a decision should practise higher-consciousness healing more often and imagine that their divine mother or father says exactly the loving things that they would have loved to hear from their biological parents. Also, they should say many loving and compassionate things to themselves during the third step (self-love), just like they would speak to a small, sad and lonely child. Generally speaking, there is not one bad quality in us that we cannot surround with a balm of love and compassion. As soon as a negative thought about ourselves arises, we simply say to ourselves, "I love myself with ... (insert here your real or imagined inadequacies)."

Envious self-comparisons with other people

Many of my clients tell me that since their kundalini awakening, they recognise more petty and hateful envy in themselves than ever before. We can attribute this development again to the opening of our subconscious mind, which forces us once again to acknowledge the not-so-nice parts of our personality. In mild cases, it will be enough to counteract these ugly tendencies with plenty of self-love and a strong determination to appreciate other people.

Some people, however, have a severe problem with envy. They constantly compare themselves with other people and concentrate too much on their own weaknesses and shortcomings. Those who have this problem should, first of all, realise that envy - with all the suffering that goes along with this attitude – is a choice we have made ourselves. Nobody forces us to compare ourselves with others - we can decide whether we want to focus on our supposed inferiority or on what we value in ourselves and others.

After we have become aware of this freedom, we should begin an internal discipline to turn away from all comparisons with other people and only ever compare ourselves to ourselves. So, we should try to gauge how much progress we have made in the last few days, weeks or years in different areas of our lives. We can also imagine that we are on a path towards our higher consciousness who is sitting on top of a high mountain. Sometimes our path is easy and at other times we have to overcome rocky cliffs and scree slopes. Everyone has their own unique path to their higher consciousness and it does not matter whether other people are faster or slower on their own paths than we are. The only thing that matters is that we move forward the best we can and that we appreciate ourselves for every step we take.

It may be useful to write down once or twice a year the progress we have made and then try to appreciate it without allowing ourselves to compare it with other people's progress. We can compare this discipline of keeping our mind on constructive thoughts with healthy eating. No matter how tempting it is to eat all those unhealthy things, we know that we would feel terrible if we gave in to our greed. It is the same with envy: it is possible to turn our mind away from this form of negative thinking if we are determined to let go from this negative habit.

A second way to transform envy is to see it as a sign that points to our own desires. There are, for example, some (spiritual) people who firmly believe that they neither desire nor need to have a partner, physical beauty or material possessions. Nevertheless, they are suddenly overcome by a malicious and hateful feeling when they see a beautiful, happily married couple in their spiritual centre who also seem to be quite rich. In such a case, they should smile towards themselves and try to admit that they are not quite as happy and content as they thought they were. In the second step, they should then try to achieve in their own lives what they feel envious of in others. In this way, envy becomes a useful motivator to improve our lives.

Negative thinking about the world
Those who are inclined to negative thinking about other people and the world in general and see themselves as victims of a "bad world" should do

155

the following gratitude exercise daily. This exercise can also be done well with another person, for example with our partner, and is a wonderful mood lifter.

Gratefulness exercise

Start by listing everything good that you are grateful for in your life.

Now go to the things that you normally take for granted, for instance, that you have been born in a free country or that you have two healthy legs. Tell yourself that you are grateful for these things.

Gradually try to include things that you do not like in yourself and in other people and try to find a reason why you can be thankful for these things. Painful experiences can help us to develop more compassion, for example, and adverse circumstances can help us to practise patience or reduce bad karma.

Hateful and aggressive thoughts

During the kundalini process, many people discover hateful, racist, sexist and other unpleasant thoughts in themselves, which can be a bit shocking if we previously considered ourselves to be "good people". However, these thoughts do not need to scare us because we do not need to believe them, let alone act them out. For our proud "spiritual ego", it may be actually quite good to get a dampener because these thoughts make us realise that we have no guarantee of our "goodness" and that it requires perpetual mindfulness to keep our aggressive tendencies under control.

Some people feel guilty when they notice such horrible thoughts within themselves. But this guilt is not necessary as long as we do not express these thoughts in any way. We should also realise that it is possible that we may have "snapped up" these thoughts from other people in our environment because our minds function as both antennae and transmitters. The nasty idea in our head can either come from our own subconscious mind, from the person standing next to us or even from the person to whom the nasty remark is aimed at because this person may be having inferior thoughts about themselves.

156

In my experience, is it almost impossible to determine exactly where our thoughts come from and it is not necessary to know this anyway. It is only important that we respond with compassion towards ourselves and towards the victim of our inner, ugly remarks. In this way, we can use such thoughts as a trigger for spiritual practice, which can only be of benefit for everyone. If someone is good at dealing with ugly impulses, they can also try to channel them into a refreshing sense of humour. We just need to be careful that our aggressiveness does not poison the humour.

When hateful thoughts take over, it is certainly a sign that we should meditate more on love and compassion and practise higher-consciousness healing more often.

Compulsive thinking and ruminating

Anyone who tends to dwell obsessively on problems and worries will notice that this tendency, too, will increase in the kundalini process. The solution to this problem starts with understanding that the ruminating in itself is the main problem and not the subject about which we are brooding. We should, therefore, meditate more and try to think and talk less.

Unfortunately, I know that this advice is not easy to implement for the compulsive ruminator because they are hoping to find solutions for their problems through their endless reflections and it is therefore not easy to give it up. Here it is important to apply the higher-consciousness method again and again and direct it towards the people who we are thinking compulsively about. For example, if we have frequent imaginary discussions with certain people, we should try to visualise them in bubbles of love every single time these thoughts come up until these compulsive tendencies subside. If we are constantly thinking with great anxiety about the future, we should practise the anti-anxiety exercise and learn to visualise a positive vision of the future. If we reflect again and again with great sorrow about all the things that we have missed out on in the past, we should frequently use the gratefulness exercise that I described earlier in this section in order to be able to appreciate our present more.

If the compulsion to ruminate is really strong, we can also try to help ourselves by reciting a mantra until our thoughts subside. Mantras are words or short phrases that we simply repeat to ourselves quietly or loudly in order to replace our ruminating. We can use for this purpose well-known mantras like "Om Mani Padme Hum" or phrases we create ourselves, for example, "love and happiness for all".

"Taking on" negative feelings and problems from other people

Many of my clients complain that they "absorb" negative things from other people, even though they do not want to. These may be other people's feelings, thoughts or even illnesses. To deal with this issue constructively, we should first make it clear to ourselves that we are literally made up of mental "material" that other people have put into us. This starts first of all with language because without language we would, mentally, be very much like an animal. And all language comes from other people mixed up with the values and taboos of our prevailing culture. Whether it suits our ego or not, language - and therefore its content - is only "passed around". It does not come out of ourselves, just like nothing else is uniquely our own. We are literally composed of the influences of other people. Our unique individuality arises only from the particular mixture of influences to which we were unconsciously or unintentionally exposed to or to which we have consciously opened up.

The average person will now probably insist that, surely, he or she is special and has a unique "soul" or "core". Unfortunately, those who think this way are even more likely to become victims of the intense influences that we are all exposed to daily through advertising, the media and our entire culture with their respective taboos. Only the more conscious person will see the need to think things through themselves to avoid, at least partially, this constant brainwashing. Nevertheless, it is difficult even for them to question the overarching belief systems of their entire culture and therefore create the possibility of radically exposing themselves to different influences.

In the kundalini process, many people can directly experience how their minds literally mingle with the minds of other people and how they suddenly begin to experience the emotions of others as their own or recognise in themselves thoughts that are definitely not wanted by themselves. This can also happen on a large scale when whole "clouds" of emotions go around the world and trigger strong, unfamiliar emotions in people. For example, it is interesting to see how many people can remember exactly what they were doing when they heard the news of Lady Diana's death and how (surprisingly) sad they were about it - as if she was a personal relative. Phenomena like global trends, ideas that appear simultaneously in different parts of the world and mass hysteria can also be explained by this dynamic.

The realisation of how much we are mixed up with the mental contents of other people may be shocking if someone believes that their mind ceases at their body boundaries and that the thoughts in their head are always their own ideas. Realising that this is not the case should encourage us to make clearer decisions to whom and to what we want to open ourselves up to or from whom we want to shut ourselves off. As previously described, my kundalini clients as a group have a general tendency to be too surrendered and uncritical, which unfortunately only aggravates this situation.

The best way to deal with this dynamic is to surrender solely to our higher consciousness while staying critical (but compassionate) towards other people. We can strengthen this attitude through practising higher-consciousness healing. In the first step, we emphasise the devotion to our higher consciousness and then we set clear boundaries by visualising the bubble around ourselves in the second step. In the final step, we visualise other people in their bubbles and make clear statements as described in the anti-anger exercise. The stronger our determination to deal with people in this way, the less likely it is that we will inadvertently pick up unwanted material from them.

It is also important to understand that the dynamic of taking on material from other people is especially strong if we ourselves have a tendency in the direction of these feelings. For example, we will take on more fears or depression from other people if we ourselves have a tendency towards fear and depression. For this reason, these problems are also an invitation to work on our own negative tendencies.

159

Taking on unwanted material from others can happen particularly easily if the other person tries to hide their true feelings, for example, when they pretend to be happy when, in truth, they are feeling quite depressed at that moment. Therefore, we should always try to notice when a sudden change of mood correlates with meeting a certain person. But as I have described above, we should avoid blaming this person for this situation but understand that the unwanted transference could only have happened because we ourselves have a tendency towards this negative material. In the next step, we can work with higher-consciousness healing on this problem.

Once we have learnt to wilfully close off from the mental influences of others, we can also learn to open up deliberately to more positive and inspired influences - such as a spiritual teacher. Learning to mingle our mind with the mind of a more advanced being will greatly accelerate our spiritual progress.

Signs and omens

A number of my clients told me about unusual number combinations that they see again and again or similar things such as feathers that came from angels or experiences in nature that appeared to be supernatural. As long as these signs and omens are positive and inspire our spiritual practice, we do not need to worry about them and we can just enjoy them.

Problems arise when we begin to be scared by such signs or when we attribute to them too much power and influence over our lives. If this happens, we should make it clear to ourselves that signs and omens are always dependent on our interpretation and that any interpretation is always dependent on our state of mind. So, when we are anxious and depressed, the signs we see will probably point to threats and dark things. But if we feel happy and optimistic, we will most likely interpret the same signs more positively. Ultimately, it all comes back to the principle that we should strive to lift our state of mind to the highest level and, if we succeed, we will not need any more signs and omens because the whole world will appear to us as an expression of our higher consciousness.

In general, I advise caution on this issue because the risk of becoming involved in dark, paranoid fantasies is not insignificant. There is also the danger of being misled by such signs into irrational decisions. As I described in the third chapter, my clients as a group tend to trust their intuition too much and give away too much of their personal power in the process. Unfortunately, I have seen cases where this imbalance has led to unhealthy choices, particularly when choosing a partner or when making financial decisions.

Conspiracy theories

Since the Internet's existence, more and more people have become involved in conspiracy theories and I have also had a number of kundalini clients who were more or less compulsively involved in these ideas. They all experienced a considerable amount of suffering through this involvement. All conspiracy theories have in common that they believe in a dark, invisible force that somehow intends to harm us normal beings. It is relatively unimportant whether this force is seen as the Illuminati, reptiles hiding in people, aeroplanes spraying chemicals or anything else. Unfortunately, all conspiracy theories have the disadvantage that one can neither prove nor refute them and this is true even if they have millions of followers on the Internet who see "signs" of their conspiracy theory everywhere. Because of this dynamic, people make themselves helpless victims as soon as they get involved in these theories.

The evil from which all conspiracy theories report - the dark, invisible force that wants to dominate and harm us - does exist but in a form that is visible and provable. We do not need to believe in the Illuminati, reptiles or the old-fashioned devil because we can see those dark forces in the overt or covert narcissism, in the lies and egoism of the people around us. Narcissistic, psychopathic or sociopathic personality disorders are a thoroughly researched fact that brings great suffering to others and people with these conditions are everywhere: in the government, in the medical profession and in the highest ranks of the church hierarchy. Even our neighbour could be a psychopath and one day shock us with frightening deeds.

As I described earlier, my clients as a group have a strong resistance to judge other people and find it very hard to see hostility and evil in other people. This "blindness" contributes to the dynamic of getting entangled in unprovable conspiracy theories instead of recognising the malignancy where it actually exists - namely, in their fellow human beings who present themselves as proverbial wolves in sheep's clothing.

It would, therefore, be wise to renounce unprovable conspiracy theories and, instead, deal with the facts of our own narcissism and the egoism of other people around us. And because these things are fact-based, we can really make a positive difference if we decide to take action. However, if we want to continue believing in conspiracy theories, we literally make ourselves into helpless victims who are at the mercy of "evil" without being able to defend ourselves against it.

Most of my clients react positively towards these explanations and conspiracy theories often quickly lose their fascination.

Dual souls or twin souls

The theory of dual or twin souls is not really a conspiracy theory but believing in this concept has similar negative consequences to believing in a conspiracy theory. I have had many clients with this problem. The twin soul (or twin flame) theory states that there is one - and only one - human being on this planet who is our predetermined dual soul and should be with us according to our life plan. It is said that the best way to recognise this human being is that they trigger an emotional "earthquake" in us.

As with most conspiracy theories, no one can really tell where this twin flame theory actually comes from and it also turns us into helpless victims. Two keywords of this personal disempowerment are "pre-destined" and "life-plan" because it remains unclear who worked out this plan and why it is now forced upon us. By comparison, the term "law of karma" is not a form of predestination but simply means "cause and effect," which is a dynamic that one can easily observe and prove in every-day life.

Most of my clients who believe in twin souls have, unfortunately, the problem that their respective dual flames are not interested in a

162

relationship with them. They, therefore, often suffer deeply because they have created a trap for themselves through their belief that there is only one twin flame for them. Things get even more complicated if the supposed twin flame has triggered a kundalini awakening in my client and they, therefore, believe even more strongly that this person must be incredibly special and irreplaceable for them. However, I have observed that a kundalini awakening is often triggered by intense love feelings that have not been sexually consummated. In other words, the kundalini awakening can feel like an earthquake but it can be triggered by a quite ordinary person. It is the withholding of sex combined with the feeling of being in love that produces the amazing expansion of consciousness.

I encourage my clients to understand the long-term effects of believing in twin flames and that these effects are all very negative. I also advise them to believe only in spiritual concepts that have long-term positive effects for all involved. The concept of the dual soul is certainly not one of them.

Paranormal experiences

Paranormal experiences are all sorts of phenomena that do not fit into our normal view of the world. They can be positive and constructive or scary and confusing. Here is a small selection of such experiences:

Visions
Telepathy
Communication with deceased people
Incredible and extremely improbable "coincidences"
Seeing ghosts
Spiritual healing
Premonitions
Clairvoyance
Hearing voices
Communication with divine beings

These experiences are often mocked, denied or labelled with a psychiatric diagnosis by people without kundalini. This can be annoying, lonely and scary for someone who has these experiences. It is as if most humans are colour-blind and only people with a kundalini awakening can see colours. Sometimes they tell the colour-blind people about their experiences but they respond by saying, "Nonsense, that is all imagination. Everyone knows that there are no colours and that this is just a myth or a hallucination." It does not matter how often the people with expanded consciousness repeat that they can see colours, the colour-blind people will react at best with mild indifference and at worst with aggression.

Where do paranormal experiences come from?

In our prevailing scientific view of the world, the law of the subject-object separation applies. This means that I, like a scientist, (subject) can observe my object of investigation objectively without influencing or changing it. When it comes to natural sciences such as physics and chemistry, this approach has many advantages and has brought many useful scientific insights. In other scientific disciplines such as quantum physics, psychology or research into the effectiveness of drugs, the subject-object separation comes to its limit. In quantum physics, the smallest particles behave in different ways when they are observed compared to when they are not observed. In psychology, it is extremely difficult to conduct objective experiments and when it comes to the research of the efficacy of drugs, the researcher is constantly confronted with the interference of the placebo effect.

In the world of the paranormal, there is less or even no separation between the subject (me) and the object (the paranormal pheno-menon). This means that whatever happens in the paranormal world takes place on the outside but is simultaneously a part of our minds. If you now get a knot in your head, please remember the hourglass personality model which is open at the top and the bottom. When our mind is expanded enough, we can become clairvoyant and get into contact with higher beings through the opening at the top. Alternatively, we can access the content of the subconscious minds of other people through the bottom part. Without the expansion of consciousness, all this stays invisible. So, by expanding our mind we can perceive in our *own* mind what belongs to the minds of *other* people or beings. This can be thought of as two circles which partially overlap and produce an interface in which the content belongs to both circles.

It is also possible to predict the future, heal diseases and manifest desires through this expansion of consciousness. These are wonderful skills - the so-called siddhis - and I will say a little more about them at the end of the book. You can also read about manifesting your desires in my book *Advanced Manifesting*. In this book here, I will continue focusing on curing problematic kundalini symptoms, so I will focus mainly on the fears and confusion around this subject.

Frightening paranormal experiences can be very strong and they are different from mere "illusions" in that they have an undeniable sense of realness about them. However, they are not mental illnesses and I have already explained in the first chapter how these experiences differ from true psychoses and schizophrenia. Therefore, I would like only to repeat briefly that you are *not* mentally ill in a clinical sense as long as you know that you are having experiences that the general world view would class as "abnormal". The ability to make this distinction represents your mental health. In other words, during a paranormal experience, a mental dimension has been *added* to your normal sense of reality, while in a genuine psychosis the normal sense of reality has been lost and people often behave inappropriately or endanger themselves. Nonetheless, unwelcome paranormal experiences can be very scary and confusing.

How to deal positively with unwelcome paranormal experiences
No matter what kind of unwelcome paranormal experiences we have and no matter how lifelike and realistic they are - whether we hear voices, are contacted by "demons" or perceive ominous omens - it is of utmost importance that we always interpret these experiences as coming from our unconscious mind. If other beings are present in our paranormal experiences, it is important to understand that this can only take place if we have given them (unconscious) permission to contact us. The

following guidelines apply:

Paranormal experiences can never (objectively) exist solely from their own side. They always need our participation or permission to appear in our perception.

Paranormal experiences can only continue to manifest in our mind as long as we give them our attention and therefore the permission and the energy to continue to exist.

Once we consistently stop giving our attention to paranormal experiences, they will disappear.

Astral (paranormal) beings are always weaker than us because they only live through our attention.

In some religions or spiritual paths, there is a belief that we can be "possessed" by demons and other terrible beings. It is of utmost importance that we reject these ideas and, instead, adopt the concept that all these phenomena are our own "unconscious material" or our "sub-personalities" or, at the very least, that astral beings can only contact us because we have (unconsciously) permitted them to do so. As soon as we adopt this self-responsible attitude, we will notice that our fear of such experiences decreases significantly. By contrast, people who want to continue believing in genuine autonomous astral beings who contact them without their permission or even possess them, take a risk with their sanity.

To end unwelcome paranormal experiences, we must divert our attention from these phenomena, because, as I have explained, they can only exist through our attention. We do this by focusing fully and completely on our higher consciousness. We should try to visualise every little detail of our deity and imagine the light that emanates from them. So, it is all about concentrating so much that our mind is completely filled with the visualisation and not a single ounce of attention is left for the unwelcome paranormal phenomena.

If you have auditory phenomena (such as hearing voices), it is useful to say a little prayer like the one I recommended in the section on waking in the morning. You can, for example, repeat "divine Mother, I take refuge in you." It is good to say this prayer loudly so that the voices and other auditory phenomena are drowned out.

For most people, it is enough to focus in this way for only 10 to 20 seconds until the unwelcome paranormal phenomenon has subsided. However, it is often necessary to repeat this little exercise from time to time until these experiences stop completely. With the attitude that these phenomena come from our unconscious mind, most of my clients were able to shut down these experiences quickly or at least learnt not to be scared by them anymore.

In rare cases, people can feel haunted by a very specific paranormal being. If this happens, I advise them again to assume that they un-consciously gave this being permission to get in contact with them. Some clients also report that they had consciously given the being permission (for example, an angel or a spiritual guide) because they hoped for help from them and later found that the being became "evil" and tried to dominate them instead of helping them.

When this happens, I advise them to deal with this being in the same way that I described in the section about anger. So, they visualise this being in a ball between the hands of their higher power, wish them to be healed and imagine that they get filled with divine light until they come to their senses. Finally, they see how their higher power carries the being away until it is completely out of their field of vision. When they have finished this visualisation, they can go back to the short prayer practice or they can follow the other steps of higher-consciousness healing.

Since all unwelcome paranormal experiences come from our own mind, we should also work pre-emptively to prevent them from appearing in the first place. We do this by "ordering" our unconscious mind that we only want to have positive paranormal experiences that will help us on our spiritual path. We may have to repeat this order a few times but, if we are serious and determined, we will be successful in stopping all unwelcome paranormal experiences after some time. The duration of this time depends on how deeply ingrained our habit is. I would like to reiterate at this point that repeated unwelcome paranormal experiences can only happen because we have given our permission to let them happen and that, therefore, we also have the power to shut them down.

At this point, one might wonder if my recommendations amount to simply suppressing unwelcome paranormal experiences. The answer is that we should not suppress these experiences but we should *ignore* them, which makes an important difference. We do not deny what we are experiencing but we say that we simply have no interest in these appearances. In my experience, it does not make much sense to work psychologically at this level, for example, by engaging with a demon in dialogue or taking a closer look at the horror visions. The danger of being traumatised by these very realistic and horrific inner experiences is not insignificant.

It is also very difficult to connect our personal psychological material with these unwelcome experiences as long as they have been split off into paranormal experiences. For example, if we repress our anger too much (and therefore, "splitting it off" from our conscious mind), this rage may appear as a "demon" next to our bed at night and will terrify us. In my work, it has been shown that it is better to rigorously ignore these phenomena until the anger (or whatever has been split off) appears clearer in our mind as our own emotion. Once this emotion surfaces, we can work with it with higher-consciousness healing.

Once we have learned to deal confidently with the paranormal world, we can then consciously open ourselves to its positive and constructive influences. I myself have done this, for example, with my myriad of questions to my own higher consciousness White Tara. In this way, I gained much spiritual knowledge that I now use to help other people through my books and my counselling. In my personal life too, the ability to communicate with White Tara has helped me tremendously and continues to do so virtually every day.

Dealing with "psychic attacks" from other people

In my opinion, we do not need to be afraid of psychic attacks or black magic from other people. To work successfully with black magic, a person needs a high degree of spiritual knowledge, a high ability to concentrate and a cruel desire to use these skills to the detriment of other people. In my experience, such a combination exists only very rarely. In the unlikely event that we become a victim of black magic and we suspect a specific person, we can proceed in the same way as described in the section on anger.

However, it may be possible that we can sense when someone else close to us feels aggressive envy or hatred towards us. These are not real psychic attacks because these people would not even know how to do that. They are just mad at us and we can feel that through our increased sensitivity. In these cases, too, we can just work with higher-consciousness healing as described in the section about anger until our symptoms subside.

It is important that we do not fall into self-pity when we experience things like this but that we understand that we ourselves have set into motion this negative dynamic at some point in time and that this is now karmically coming back to us. For that reason, we now have a precious opportunity to clean up some of our old bad karma.

We should also always consider the possibility that what we think is a psychic attack is just our own material that rises up from our unconscious mind. We can then simply work on these symptoms as described in the previous chapters. At the end of the day, it does not really matter whether our symptoms come from our unconsciousness or are triggered by a psychic attack because we can resolve all these symptoms simply with higher-consciousness healing.

Guru Rinpoche, the founder of Tibetan Buddhism, was according to legend, frequently attacked by demons that existed in Tibet at that time. He confidently declared that these attacks were like firewood, only fuelling his enlightenment process. In the same way, we can use all our problems on our kundalini path - including psychic attacks - as firewood for our enlightenment. This is especially true for real black magic attacks because it takes a huge amount of energy to send evil wishes to us. Once we have transformed the negative energy with higher-consciousness healing, we can keep the energy and use it for ourselves. It is rather like someone throws a stone at us that is made of diamonds. It hurts a bit but afterwards, we can keep the diamonds. Psychic attacks are, therefore, basically a gift. If you know how to deal with these attacks, they will make us only stronger and not weaker.

Fear of egolessness

One special anxiety that some people have in the kundalini process is the fear that they "have to" let go of their ego and then become a "nothing". This fear often results from listening to misleading spiritual teachings that misrepresent Hindu or Buddhist teachings about the ego. For example, in these teachings, there is mention of "ego death" or the need to "shatter" or "crush" the ego. This violent language alone can be frightening but is, in my opinion, only a recognition that sometimes we have to deal with very egotistical people in a very strict way. It is certainly not an indication that we should become a "nothing" because that would be like recommending a mental suicide.

I had a client who was a disciple of a rather famous Indian guru who told me that he taught that we should be become "nothing". Apparently, he described the voluntary chosen death of his wife through meditation (mahasamadhi) as a wonderful example what his teachings were all about. My client was in total despair because these teaching worsened her self-hatred and depression since everything in her life felt now completely meaningless. It never occurred to her that the "mahasamadhi" of this woman might have been just a glamorised but actually ordinary suicide and that a guru can control his students better if they are trying to be "nothing" and have an "empty mind". The teacher himself actually behaved not at all like a "nothing". He lived in luxury, rode an expensive motorcycle through the ashram and financed his daughter a glamorous life that she proudly showed off on Instagram.

The truth is that we always maintain our willpower - even in the highest spiritual states - and thereby we will always maintain a sense of self. This enlightened sense of self is called Buddha-nature in Tibetan Buddhism and we have reached it when we can experience ourselves as our meditation deity with an all-pervading sense of love and bliss. So, we are not losing our sense of self on our spiritual journey but we are just losing our egotism

170

and our illusions about our limitations. In other words, we are broadening our ability to include more and more beings in our altruistic intentions. An enlightened being is, therefore, not a "nothing" that sits around in a lifeless state. On the contrary, enlightenment (or union with God) is a state in which supreme love is harmoniously combined with supreme power and people in this state are usually very active in helping others. This is the Tibetan Buddhist understanding of enlightenment.

Our mind cannot be broken or destroyed as some people fear in their despair. On the contrary, our mind is indestructible because it is just a vessel in which our thoughts and feelings take place. No matter how depressed, chaotic and frightening our thoughts and feelings are, our mind itself will always remain untouched. We can sense this untouchability when we practise observing the contents of our mind rather than identifying with them. The observer always stays outside and in times of extreme inner turmoil, I recommend practicing this "witness consciousness". Once you get a little more stable, you can begin the higher-consciousness healing and practise the anti-anxiety exercise.

Exercise: Witness consciousness (for times of extreme inner turmoil)
Relax *as much as possible and imagine that the contents of your mind are like animals in a zoo. Some animals are scary, others are disgusting and some are just annoying.*

Watch *the animals from the safe distance of the visitor's path. You do not need to be afraid because a deep ditch or a safety fence will separate you from the animals.*

Make it *clear to yourself that you are not the animal but just the observer. No matter how wild, confused and aggressive the animals (your feelings) are, you as the observer remain unaffected by all the commotion. So, never climb into the animal enclosures.*

Once you *have calmed down a bit, start the higher-consciousness healing.*

Horror visions

Many people in the kundalini process occasionally have what I call horror visions. These can be memories of something that they have read or seen somewhere or it could be an imaginary hellish scene. It may also be things like imaginary taunting voices or terrible visions of self-mutilation.

Some of my clients are badly affected by these painful phenomena and, unfortunately, there are therapists who deal with this in completely wrong ways. For example, one of my clients who suffered from terrible self-mutilation fantasies was recommended by his therapist to feel and express anger instead. I am sure that this advice was well-intentioned but, as a result, my client developed terrible aggressive fantasies in which he saw himself torturing and killing other people. He could not rid himself of these aggressive fantasies either and so developed two problems instead of one. Also, his depression became much worse because he was a Buddhist and these torture fantasies induced terrible feelings of guilt. This was another example of how some traditional therapy approaches make kundalini clients worse rather than better.

To heal horror visions, we work in the same way as we do with unwanted paranormal phenomena. In the first step, we assume that these images arise from our unconsciousness so that we do not become afraid that they come from outside and then feel even more like a victim.

In the next step, we place our mind with complete concentration onto our higher consciousness and try to visualise every little detail of their face, ornaments and clothing. It also helps to repeat a short prayer or mantra such as, "divine mother, I take refuge in you". If you are very scared, you should also practise the anti-anxiety breathing as described in the fifth chapter. If you work in this way, it may take ten to twenty seconds for the horror vision to subside again. With time, you can also learn to recognise these terrible thoughts when they are still in the shadow area of your mind. You then immediately apply the antidote and, with time, you will become able to defeat these visions even faster. Some people have such terrible visions for many years but since they are so easy to turn off, this does not need to be a big problem.

If you have aggressive fantasies, you should also ask yourself whether

172

there is an area in your life where you do not assert yourself enough. For example, my client had an 18-year-old son who often rebelled against the authority of his parents - just like any typical teenager- and he and his wife could not control him well. It was a relatively small and "normal" problem that could never have caused his terrible fantasies. Still, I encouraged my client to be more assertive with his son, which he did.

My client had suffered badly from horror visions for many years. At the beginning of our sessions, his suffering was at ten on a scale from zero to ten. Within a few months, he could reduce his suffering to one on the scale. He was able to go back to work, became creative, went regularly to his Buddhist centre and was a much happier person all round. The terrible thoughts still came back from time to time but he was always able to "shut them down" quickly.

Disturbed body perception

In the kundalini process, many people occasionally have experiences of disturbed body awareness. It could be, for example, that we perceive a body part as greatly enlarged or not at all. These are all harmless phenomena that we should not attach much importance to because they are likely to quickly pass as long as we do not become fixated on them. We must never forget that our attention in itself is a powerful instrument that we can use to increase phenomena by zooming in on them or that we can use to starve phenomena by withdrawing our attention until they disappear.

Body dysmorphia

A bigger problem is body dysmorphia which is the feeling of being too fat, ugly or somehow deformed even though these perceptions do not correspond to reality. Anyone in the kundalini process who has tendencies in this direction will experience that these, too, become enlarged and more bothersome. I have had many clients with this problem, which is why I include it here in the catalogue of kundalini symptoms.

The first point I want to make is that, in my experience, body

173

dysmorphia occurs more often the more beautiful and attractive a person is in an objective sense. This sounds paradoxical at first sight but it is easy to explain. If you are really beautiful and attractive, you will receive much positive attention and other benefits from other people. For this reason, attractive people often get attached to their advantage and make it into an ego strategy. This applies, by the way, for all the other talents that people have as well. Very intelligent people often make their superior intelligence into their main ego strategy and may neglect the development of their other skills while aggressive people may also make this "ability" into their main strategy to get through life.

But all ego strategies have the same disadvantage: ultimately, they do not work. We are never beautiful, intelligent or strong enough to feel completely safe. So, if we rely on physical beauty, we have to improve it all the time. We constantly need to build more muscles in the gym or undergo yet another beauty treatment. While we are doing all this, we are critically examining ourselves in the mirror and our self-confidence will become less and less because we mostly focus on our shortcomings. This is the reason why so many objectively beautiful people find themselves ugly.

To overcome body dysmorphia it is important to realise that we mistakenly equate our self-worth with our appearance. The whole problem is not about a few wrinkles or more or less pounds in weight but about our lack of self-esteem. This problem can be effectively resolved by practising higher-consciousness healing. We should focus especially on loving ourselves *including* all our real or imagined physical defects.

This inner work should be supported by the following behavioural strategies: We should remove all mirrors in the house apart from one. In this mirror, we should look at ourselves only once or twice a day and only for about three seconds. We should also avoid looking at ourselves in any window panes or going to places like gyms where body dysmorphia is virtually cultivated. I had many clients who could reduce or eliminate this painful neurosis with these few simple measures.

Leaving the body and fear of dying
Some people experience sensations of leaving their body during the

174

kundalini process. This can be a wonderful experience but can also trigger very strong fears, especially the fear of dying. Unfortunately, on this subject too, one can find many horror stories on the Internet or in books that exacerbate these fears. For example, one can find references to a "silver thread" that connects the soul to its lifeless body during an astral journey along with the dire warning that one should be very careful that it does not tear.

I myself had many experiences of leaving my body and I also talked to many clients who had such experiences. You do not need to be any more afraid of these experiences than of having dreams when sleeping. They are, in fact, very much like a very intense and realistic waking dream. If you look closely, you can see that it only *feels as if* you are lifted out of your body and that the physical body lies beneath you only in your *inner perception*. You then have *the feeling* that you go on an astral journey with very realistic experiences. But when the telephone rings suddenly or you are disturbed in some other way, you are quickly *back in the body*. All of these are mental experiences and should be seen as such, no matter how real and intense they feel.

The biggest problem with out-of-body experiences (OBEs) is interpreting these experiences as literally leaving the body, which can lead to all sorts of fears. A woman I knew many years ago was afraid that she would leave her body in her sleep through her crown-chakra and therefore she kept herself awake for weeks. Eventually, she ended up in a psychiatric ward where she was forced to sleep through medication and, of course, she did not die. Another client of mine had very similar fears, developed a really bad sleep disorder and had to take extremely high doses of neuroleptics to manage her life. After explaining everything in detail to her, she was able (in collaboration with her psychiatrist) to remove the medication and return to her normal sleep pattern without any further problems.

Yet another client reported various unpleasant energy movements in her body, which she tried to suppress with high doses of neuroleptics. She, too, was adamant that she would die if she stopped the medication. After we established that her doctor had not given her any diagnosis of mental disease, I advised her to slowly reduce the neuroleptics (with the consent of her doctor). My client was unwilling to do this and ended the sessions with me. A year later she contacted me and told me joyfully that she had summoned up all her courage to stop her medication and allow the energy movements. Nothing terrible had happened, of course, and this woman was now very happy because she could pursue her creative hobbies again and did not need to vegetate like a zombie under the influence of neuroleptics any longer.

I have already stressed several times in this book that it is important to retain the ability to think rationally and base one's opinions on facts. If we interpret the many strange experiences that can occur during the kundalini process as coming from outside ourselves or interpret them too literally, this is often more of a danger than the experiences themselves.

Chapter eight
Relationships in the kundalini process

The kundalini process forces us to become more authentic and nowhere is this more apparent than in our relationships. Every family, every group of friends and every organisation has its taboos about what one can say and what cannot be said. For example, we may not be allowed to talk with our parents about certain things from the past because they become too upset. Maybe we cannot talk about all our problems with our friends either because we could get on their nerves. And at our football club, we must not make too many socially critical remarks because we may get mocked as a "hippy".

But in the kundalini process, we have a strong urge to say what we really think and not be silenced by all these taboos. As a result, people in the kundalini process are often criticised for being too sensitive, too critical and too demanding.

This dynamic most strongly affects our family of origin and our partner relationship. Our expansion of consciousness allows us less and less to simply sweep things under the rug even if we have done this for decades. For example, the mildly aggressive behaviour of our husband or the subtle blaming of our mother suddenly become unbearable. In the years leading up to our kundalini awakening, we may have found these things somewhat annoying but now we get severe stomach pains in the presence of our mother and become very angry at our husband. In this way, the kundalini "forces" us to improve our relationships or withdraw from them.

So, in the kundalini process, we should be prepared for intensive relationship work and quite a few endings, too. It is, for example, quite normal for us to change our circle of friends after a spiritual awakening and sometimes also our workplace due to our new interests and needs. This process may even be repeated several times throughout our life if we are on a particularly fast track of development. Of course, the loss of dear friends is never easy but we should see this development positively because it is only a mirror of our steady upward development.

It is a bit more complicated in partner relationships and with our family of origin and I advise all my clients to try to improve these relationships instead of simply breaking them off. I will give some advice about how to do this later in this chapter.

No relationships are not the solution

In past centuries but also still today, many spiritual people tried to circumvent the problem of difficult relationships by simply not having any. Instead, they tried to solely love God or attain enlightenment and hoped to escape the problems in a partner relationship in this way. I have seen this tendency quite clearly in many spiritual centres where intimate relationships were viewed as somewhat inferior to the "superior" path of celibacy.

I want to contrast this attitude with the fact that in over 30 years of my work as a psychotherapist and Buddhist teacher, I have never seen a single client who had the primary motivation of being alone. All of my clients - without exception - wanted a positive partner relationship given the choice. So, I suppose that the monk's or nun's path was a necessary evil at a time when there were no contraceptives and married women had few rights. But when we have the free choice, virtually all of us wish to have a close relationship as much as we need food, sleep and a roof over our heads. Of course, we can temporarily do without these things but not without suffering.

The idea that the celibate path leads faster to enlightenment is not true. On the contrary, Tibetan Buddhism and all other tantric spiritual paths say that enlightenment without a loving, sexual relationship is not even possible. (This is, of course, in contradiction to the fact that Tibetan Buddhism has a strong monastic culture but that is not the subject of this book.)

Couple relationships facilitate our spiritual development because they fulfil an essential need and, therefore, we do not need to waste energy suppressing our desire for human love. Secondly, couple relationships are an excellent vehicle to bring to light the deeper dysfunctions of our ego and, therefore, give us the chance to correct them. I will say more about this topic in the section about tantric relationships.

I do not want to be misunderstood on this point, however. There is no rule that everyone "must" have a relationship. I just want to point out the fact that people normally have this desire and that good relationships are conducive to spiritual development and do not hinder it.

Passively remaining in bad relationships is even less of a solution

Passively remaining in destructive relationships in which we are dominated, exploited or mistreated is always very harmful to our spiritual development. I have had many clients (they were almost exclusively women) who asked me for "tips" to decrease their suffering from living with a narcissistic partner. Unfortunately, the answer is that this is impossible. The following metaphor should explain why:

A close sexual relationship is like two buckets filled with water that are connected at the bottom with a hose that distributes the water into the two buckets. Ideally, all the water of both people in a partnership should always be distributed evenly. So, if one partner feels better than the other (and has more water), their water should flow through the hose between the buckets to the other partner until both have the same amount of water in their buckets again. This process corresponds approximately to the beautiful proverb: "a problem shared is a problem halved and a joy shared is a joy doubled". In a relationship in which one person is exploited, the dominant partner constantly draws energy away from the victim so that they have more energy (water) in their bucket. The victim always loses energy in this process, which will sooner or later lead to anger and depression and later on to psychosomatic illnesses as well. Unfortunately, no one can escape this dynamic because through regular sex it is impossible to close off completely so that the dominant partner cannot steal energy. In my experience, there is no psychotherapeutic, spiritual or energetic technique by which the victim can prevent this pattern from happening simply from their own side. No matter how much they meditate, practise forgiveness, pray for their partner or visualise protective energy balls around themselves, the energy robbery will

179

continue to take place and weaken the victim further and further.

Unfortunately, many people in the kundalini process find themselves in exactly this situation - either with their partner or with family members who do not treat them well. When the kundalini partner tries to talk about this destructive dynamic, the dominant people around them will often react with disapproval and anger, making things even worse.

My advice is to always try to improve an already existing relationship rather than simply breaking up as long as no severe addictions or violence are present. I give this advice because I consider existing relationships as precious and also for the reason that without this relationship work, it is likely that people will quickly find themselves in a similar relationship pattern with someone else. All relationship work is therefore well worth it even if we ultimately decide to split up. In the following sections, I will describe how best to go about this work and will focus mainly on partner relationships between men and women. For all other relationships, you should try to adapt this advice to your respective situations.

The tantric relationship

In her book "Passionate Enlightenment", Miranda Shaw explains that the term "tantra" in its original translation means "weaving" or "weaving together". Therefore, on the tantric path our main aim is to weave all aspects of our life together - our sexuality with our spirituality, our professional life with our spirituality, our parenting with our spirituality and all other areas of life, as well. This form of spirituality that is integrated into all areas of life was mainly practised in India from the eighth to the twelfth centuries A.D. and became known as the tantric movement. What I will write in the following section is based on Miranda Shaw's description of tantric Buddhism in medieval India.

In tantra, we try to bring the lower part of the hourglass personality model, where our (unconscious) desires for aggression, sexuality and power reside, into harmony with the higher consciousness in the upper part of the hourglass, where our wishes for love, wisdom and spirituality reside. The so-called "lower instincts" in the bottom part of the hourglass are often triggered by sex and daily conflicts in a partner relationship and may lead to arguments and, ultimately, to separation. The ideal of a tantric relationship is to transform these difficult impulses from our subconscious mind and, together with our partner, use them for spiritual development.

This classical tantric perspective should not be confused with the so-called "tantric courses" that are offered everywhere these days. Sadly, as I have heard many times from my clients, the opposite is practised on these courses compared to what is actually meant by tantra. Instead of integrating love and sexuality, they are torn apart even further, for example, by practising sexual exercises with complete strangers in a workshop. In real tantra, we try to connect love, commitment and sex more deeply, which is only possible within a committed and deeply loving partnership. In contrast, if we act out our sex-drive outside such a relationship, we tear the higher and lower chakras even further apart and deepen our most fundamental split.

Real tantra is about the transformation of our so-called "lower instincts" and using the released energy for enlightenment. This is not unlike the psychoanalytic concept of sublimating the sex drive into "culturally higher activities" such as art and science. The difference is that Sigmund Freud's idea of sublimation assumes that there will be an end to our sex drive as well as the fact that Freud did not have a high opinion of spirituality. From the tantric point of view, we need to integrate our sexuality (and all other areas of our life) harmoniously into our spirituality so that the search for God becomes the central and all-embracing goal of our life.

Tantra is therefore all about the integration of the upper and lower chakras so that the love and wisdom of the higher chakras are in harmony with the power and dynamism of the lower chakras. For many people, the desires of the lower chakras are in conflict with the more "civilized intentions" of the upper chakras - for love, spirituality and wisdom. This inner disunity is the main reason for much of our suffering. For example, we fall in love with a person who we find very sexy but the relationship breaks up because of constant power struggles. Or we have a harmonious relationship with a kind person but suffer from a lack of sexual attraction. We want to make a lot of money in our job but feel guilty because our work contributes to environmental destruction and destroys jobs. Or we have a wonderful job in a helping profession but, unfortunately, we cannot earn enough money from it to support a family. We love a person but we cannot defend ourselves against their egotistical behaviour or we claim to love someone when in truth we just want to dominate this person. All the above are examples of how our upper and lower chakras are often in conflict.

The tantric way is to resolve all these contradictions and combine power and love harmoniously. This task is not easy and will also continue our entire life in an ever-deeper way. But I think this process is worth the effort because it will reward us on the one hand with a wonderful relationship and on the other hand with rapid spiritual growth.

The man-woman dynamics in tantric relationships

We can describe the harmonisation of the upper and lower chakras as an integration of our male and female sides, as well. In this way, we attribute the powerful and power-oriented lower chakras to our male side and the finer desires for love and wisdom in the upper chakras to our female side. Since all people have all the chakras, every person has a female and a male side and we all have the same task of uniting them harmoniously no matter whether we tend towards male dominance or feminine surrender.

One might assume that in today's world of gender equality, we may have outgrown the duality that men are more power-oriented and women are more relationship-oriented. However, my experience as a psychotherapist (and as a human being) shows that, as a rule, this is unfortunately not the case at all. As soon as we are dealing with sexual and romantic relationships, the old patterns of dominant men and submissive women become evident, even when both partners are confident in their working life and strong supporters of gender equality. The only thing that seems to have changed is that male chauvinism is now acted out in a more hidden and passive-aggressive way than in days gone by. Unfortunately, this makes it even harder to fight back against it. I would say that I see this unfortunate pattern in around 97 per cent of my male and female clients.

In a tantric relationship, the main aim is that both men and women learn from each other to develop and integrate the missing part in themselves. So, women should learn from their husbands to be more confident and stronger while men should learn from their wives to be more caring and empathic. At least, that is the theory. In practice, however, it turns out that even the most spiritual men are often extremely reluctant to give up their striving for dominance and develop genuine compassion instead. I have seen this clearly when working with my clients and it was also described in this way in the tantric movement a thousand years ago in India.

Women are therefore often more willing to learn from their husbands and often become genuinely more confident and stronger as they get older. In contrast, men are often much more ambivalent about their task of becoming more empathic and loving. On the one hand, they see the need for this development but their male ego vehemently refuses to give up their old privileges. In extreme cases, such a man develops more and more envy towards their blossoming wife and experiences what is commonly described as a stereotypical mid-life crisis - a desperate attempt to salvage something from their old male superiority by perhaps buying a motorbike or taking a younger woman as a lover.

To counteract this unequal willingness to evolve spiritually, women (or the partner with the more developed feminine side) should hold the leading position in a tantric relationship and be the spiritual teacher for their partner. Both partners - the man and the woman - should voluntarily accept these roles to jointly transform the stubborn male desire to dominate. In this way, the woman is strengthened in her masculine side and the man is strengthened in his surrendering feminine side so that both partners can become more complete beings who harmoniously integrate their upper and lower chakras. The female partner should also hold the stronger position because when a dispute occurs, love should dominate power and not the other way round.

I can confirm from my twenty-two-year marriage that the tantric model

183

works wonderfully and leads to extraordinary happiness in a partnership and I have also seen this in other couples who work in the same way with each other. Unfortunately, almost all my female clients do not like the idea of a tantric relationship at first. In the rare cases in which a man has a more developed feminine side than his wife, I have often encountered even more resistance. However, when my clients try out what I am suggesting, they are often positively surprised.

Building a tantric relationship

It is quite possible to transform an existing relationship into a tantric one. For some couples, the tantric perspective can even be lifesaving. In the first step, the woman (or the man, if he has a more developed feminine side than his wife) should initiate a conversation in which both partners talk about their most important values and the deepest meaning and purpose of their partnership. This conversation aims at developing a shared world view and philosophy of life. For example, many people may agree with the idea that a marriage should serve the development of both partners so that they can both reach their highest potential. One should go as far as possible into detail and ask questions like, "what does the highest potential mean? What is spiritual development?" or "what is love? How do we recognise a loving act?", etc. Ideally, one should have the goal that the relationship should serve as a place where both partners learn in the fastest and most harmonious way to love more deeply and that all relationship difficulties should be used to achieve this goal.

If you have reached a consensus in your conversation, you should write it down and maybe frame it and hang it up in your bedroom. Part of this agreement should also be the promise to be allowed to confront each other when one partner does not keep to the agreement and to accept each other's help to grow together.

In the second step, both partners should put their promise into action and (lovingly) confront their partner when they do not keep to this agreement. As explained earlier, the two partners could theoretically alternate being the teacher to learn from each other. In practice, however, it will usually be the woman who occupies this position and has to confront her partner again and again about his open or hidden ways of trying to dominate to gain selfish advantages. These could be small manipulations, the refusal to communicate or the lack of desire to honestly research and reveal the deeper (selfish) motives behind their actions.

Ideally, the partner in the teacher position should work systematically - just like a good teacher with a curriculum. They should also consider how they can motivate their partner time and again to appreciate that these relationship agreements are worthwhile and invent methods, such as role-play, to teach their partner to have greater empathy.

As you can imagine, the implications of this advice will quickly lead to resistance and arguments even among the most well-intentioned partners. Here it is important to define some ground rules about what a relationship can carry and when it has to end. For example, physical or verbal violence, emotional cruelty or untreated addictive behaviour is incompatible with the concept of a tantric relationship. All other behaviours and relationship difficulties can be addressed and negotiated by both partners to grow together. It will require a lot of patience and stamina of both people to go through this process because no one likes their partner taking away their cherished domination strategies.

As mentioned earlier, most of my clients do not desire to live out their relationship in this way. The women explain to me, for example, that they do not want to become the teacher of their husband and do not want to have another "child" that they have to educate. However, it is important to see that the partner in the teacher position (usually the woman) can gain tremendous advantages from this approach. Firstly, one always learns best what one teaches. The woman should also understand that she needs these teachings because it is not by chance that she has ended up with a partner who has exactly those flaws that annoy her so much. His selfishness is a precise mirror image of her lack of self-confidence and by willingly taking the position of a teacher, she can now heal this deficiency. If she does her job well, she will be rewarded with a far more affectionate partner. Also, through this process, both partners will be able to grow spiritually much faster than would be possible through medi-tation alone or attending workshops.

I would even go so far as to say that the tantric relationship model is the *only* way to grow and be happy with a partner in the kundalini process. One of my Buddhist teachers always said, "if you want to measure the spiritual development of a man, just watch how he treats women." I can only agree with this statement and would add the following sentence: "if you want to measure the spiritual development of a woman, just look at how well she is treated by her husband."

Personality disorders

It is a sad fact that many of my clients have big problems with one or more people around them who have a personality disorder. I use this term here loosely and also include people who simply have traits of personality disorders. There are many different personality disorders such as narcissistic, borderline, schizoid and psychopathic disorders and I will try to summarise their similarities in the following list:

Signs of personality disorders

Pronounced egotism

Lack of empathy or ability to love and care

Frequent and sudden behavioural changes: first loving and charming, then cold and hateful

Attempt to use and exploit other people

Attempt to control and dominate other people

Use of lies and manipulations to enforce one´s own will

Using outbursts of anger and other extreme emotions to enforce one's will

Often friendly and fully functional in the outside world but selfish and hostile at home

Inability and unwillingness to talk honestly and rationally about relationship issues

Entitled attitude and double standards: expecting privileges and not giving as much back

Submitting people who are close to them to "loyalty tests" by humiliating them

Pronounced envy and pleasure in humiliating the partner as a "competitor"

Twisting the facts: presenting themselves as victims and accusing the real victim

Having an unrealistically high opinion of oneself and exaggerating all the "good" they are doing

Unwillingness to admit one's own mistakes or apologise for the shameful things one has done

Inability and unwillingness to handle criticism constructively

Inability and unwillingness to abide by agreements and promises

Constant repetition of negative behaviour, despite promising not to do it again

Many people without a kundalini awakening also suffer around human beings with personality disordered traits but my clients seem to suffer especially strongly. In my experience, they find it particularly difficult because they just cannot imagine that people can be so cruel and hateful. Due to this lack of understanding, they try to deal with these kinds of people completely wrongly and thereby exacerbate the problems.

To understand personality disorders better, it is helpful to imagine them as remnants of animal behaviour. Some animal species fight to the death for their place in the pecking order and it is the same for humans with personality disorders. These people are only concerned with one thing: to get - through any legitimate or illegitimate manner - into a position where they are "above" others and can exercise power and control. In this struggle for supremacy and domination, people with personality disorders are manipulative, domineering, deceitful, malicious and sometimes also violent.

The biggest problem for my clients is the fact that they just cannot understand why someone from their own family can be so mean and vicious when they could just as well enjoy having a loving and beautiful relationship with them. Therefore, they often incorrectly assume that they must have caused the other person's horrible behaviour by inadvertently provoking them or that the personality disordered person must have experienced a terrible trauma that causes their ugly behaviour. Both assumptions are fundamentally wrong and keep my clients in a position in which they continue to be dominated, abused and exploited by someone else.

However, in most cases you cannot provoke hateful and domineering behaviour in other people, nor can you prevent it, no matter what you do. The behaviour of the personality disordered person is largely caused by envy and the biggest "crime" you can be blamed for is to achieve more, be more beautiful or be in some other way better and superior. This, however, does not mean that you will be treated in a better way if you do not provoke this envy because the personality disordered person also regularly humiliates "inferior" people to prevent the situation ever coming to a competition.

What makes personality disordered people angry the most is when other people have a good heart. We all know the fairy tale of Cinderella in which she is tormented by her ugly stepsisters mainly because they envied her pure and good heart. Many of my clients find themselves in such a "Cinderella-like situation" in which they try incredibly hard to win the love of a person with a personality disorder (e.g. a parent, sibling or a partner) while doubting themselves more and more because they do not succeed. They simply do not realise that it is precisely their inner and outer beauty that motivates their tormentors to be so mean to them and they can hardly believe me when I try to explain the reality of the situation.

My clients also often think that hateful, manipulative people surely must have been traumatised themselves and that this causes their bad behaviour. Again, this assumption is fundamentally wrong. George Simon, an American psychotherapist and specialist for personality disorders, explains this dynamic with the example of a cat catching a mouse and torturing it with pleasure slowly to death. The cat is not traumatised and it is probably not even hungry. It just acts out of its animal instinct and people with a personality disorder act out the same animalistic instinct. In other words, their malicious and hateful behaviour gives them a sort of enjoyment.

It is irrelevant whether such a person had a painful childhood or not.

Traumas do not lead to aggression, hatred and lies but to post-traumatic stress disorder (PTSD), which mostly consists of anxiety and often depression. In comparison, personality disturbed behaviour is a primary, instinctual and animal-like impulse to dominate and humiliate others and gives the perpetrator a kind of primitive pleasure.

Of course, this enjoyment will be vehemently denied should you ask one of these people about it. It is nevertheless a fact. We can empathise a little bit with this pleasure by thinking of the saying, "revenge is sweet". The personality disturbed person tries, so to speak, to take revenge on the whole world because it does not give them the extreme status and the infinite power that they believe they are entitled to in their megalomaniac delusion. In a practical way, such a person takes out their envy and revenge on their partner and their children.

It is hard to empathise with this incredible unfairness but it is exactly why so many people get stuck in hurtful relationships with these people. For the same reason, many of my clients find it hard to really accept my explanation and instead have a strong tendency to "psycho-analyse" their tormentors - finding excuses for their bad behaviour and otherwise "rationalising their behaviour away". They do not realise, unfortunately, that their emotional state gets worse and worse in this process and that their fears and depression increase. To get better, it is extremely important to understand that a personality disorder is not a psychological problem and therefore cannot be explained and improved with psychological models and techniques. Personality disorders are not psychological issues but a form of *moral* misconduct, which means that the person does not know the difference between good and evil or does not want to know. In other words, people who behave in these ways do not have a properly functioning conscience.

The best way to help a person with personality disordered traits is to confront their selfishness but one should not expect to be thanked for it. On the contrary, the disordered person will try everything to cause more confusion and to convince us that they really have a "psychological pro-blem". In many cases, they will also display strong emotions like temper tantrums that look like the person is "losing it" but in reality, this is only just another strategy to dominate their victim and not a loss of control at all. This fact is well described and documented in Lundy Bancroft's book, "Why does he do that?" about domestic violence. Many experiments in prisons also have shown that psychotherapy makes these problems worse because it teaches the disordered person more skilful communication strategies that they can use to manipulate other people even more effectively. Therefore, these days many personality disturbed people are quite adept at "explaining" their problematic behaviour with psychological concepts, which makes it even harder to deal with their domineering and manipulative strategies.

The same dynamic happens in many spiritual groups too, where, sadly, we can also find many personality disordered people. Cleverly, these people twist spiritual teachings to serve their own selfish goals. For example, they may first subtly dominate and humiliate a person and if this person tries to fight back, they attack them for having "too much ego". Or, if a wife demands from her husband to help more with the household chores, he criticises her for having "control issues" or an inability to be "completely relaxed in the here-and-now". Unfortunately, spiritual teachers can have personality disorders, too, and the many scandals around sex-addicted and exploitative gurus and priests are evidence of this sad fact.

The psychiatric literature clearly states that personality disorders are largely resistant to medical and psychological treatment and for this reason little gets taught about this topic in counselling and psychotherapy training courses. Therefore, many therapists do not know enough about this issue and often treat people with these traits wrongly. This is particularly damaging in couple therapy because an "impartial" therapist inadvertently strengthens the (covertly) aggressive partner through their lack of confrontation and thus ensnares the victim even more deeply in self-doubt and low self-esteem. Unfortunately, there are also many authors who keep spreading misinformation around this subject. One example is Marie-France Hirigoyen who claims in her bestselling book "Stalking the Soul" that the bad behaviour of personality disordered people comes from their traumas.

190

If you want to seek therapeutic help with these problems, you should always ask directly whether the potential therapist is qualified in dealing with personality disorders. The most appropriate form of therapy is cognitive behavioural therapy (CBT) because it helps the disordered person to correct the illusory, megalomaniac and entitled thought patterns that they use to justify their bad behaviour. Another good method is a 12-step group - such as in Alcoholics Anonymous - which teaches the personality disordered person to take responsibility and stop blaming other people for their own wrongdoings.

In Tibetan Buddhism, these problems are referred to as "the three poisons of the mind" - hatred, greed and ignorance. To eliminate these three poisons, all forms of meditation that increase self-knowledge and love are appropriate. But one should not hope for rapid progress with any of these methods because personality disorders are like an addiction that the affected person will give up only extremely reluctantly. One can even corrupt meditation for selfish purposes by using it as a sedative or to strengthen one's ego to seem "oh, so enlightened" so that everyone must now bow down to this person. It is also common for people with personality disorders to compete with other meditation practitioners for teacher positions by using the usual lies, manipulations and power games. All charlatans – big and small - and evil cult leaders use this dynamic.

Dealing with personality disordered people

Personality disordered behaviour is on a spectrum - starting with what could be kindly described as "immature" up to full-blown psycho-pathy. What I am describing in this section should only be applied to mild personality disorders and you should quickly bring yourself to safety in the event of real cruelty and violence.

The first and most important step in dealing with these problems is to understand and correct the misconceptions about personality disorders, which I have described in the section above. It helps to learn more about these conditions and read books like those of George Simon that clearly explain the true causes of this difficult behaviour. Because my clients as a

191

group have an aversion to judging others, this often represents a challenge for them. But we are not trying to condemn these people as terrible devils or something similar. We can and should make our judgments always with compassion and should never forget that personality disordered people also have a divine nature. It is only more deeply buried than in more mature people. However, we need to avoid falling into the trap of thinking that the personality disturbed person suffers and somehow wants to be freed from their pain. Nothing could be further from the truth. All lies, all meanness and all selfish behaviours are motivated by the pleasure and enjoyment that the personality disturbed person feels when they are acting in this way.

The best way to free yourself from the confusion and entanglement with a personality disordered person is to apply higher-consciousness healing as described in the anti-anger exercise in the fifth chapter. As explained in the exercise, you should mentally tell the person what they have done wrong (e.g. "you are an exploitative, deceiving narcissist") and then you say, "I stop grudging you now and I wish you to be healed". In this way, you unite liberating clarity with wisdom and compassion. You then visualise the personality disturbed person in a bubble of light between the hands of a large higher power and you see how the divine light fills this person from the bottom up. When the light reaches their forehead, the person sees themselves as they really are without any excuses. I have seen countless times that this exercise has helped my clients to free themselves from their confusion, their helpless anger and their lack of self-confidence.

The second step is to confront the personality disturbed person in real life (obviously only if this is safe). If this person is your partner, you should also try to implement the tantric relationship model if possible. Even though the chances are slim that these approaches will change a personality disordered person, it is still important that at least we give it a try. Through this relationship work and the attempt to communicate our truth more clearly, we grow as people and gain more self-confidence. It is not an easy job but it is a very important one since otherwise there is a strong risk of repeating the same pattern with similarly disturbed people over and over again.

If you ultimately conclude that any further confrontations are futile, you need to distance yourself from these people in the third step. This can often be difficult to do if you have been very close to this person. When practising higher-consciousness healing, it will help if you push the ball of the other person further away until you find the distance that feels just right. If you want to completely separate yourself from the other person, you should push the ball over the horizon until it disappears.

It is especially hard to separate from abusive parents when their destructiveness is so great that you cannot even maintain a distant, polite relationship with them. In such a case, you should always keep in mind that your real parents are your divine father and your divine mother. These heavenly parents will care for you forever with perfect love while your biological parents come and go in your different lifetimes. So, you should try to get parental love from your higher consciousness and I have seen in my work with thousands of clients that this works beautifully and perfectly heals all wounds from a bad childhood.

Dealing with your own personality disturbed traits

It is not so rare that during a kundalini process, anti-social and domineering impulses emerge or that an already existing mild personality disorder gets significantly worse. For example, you may suddenly discover shockingly sexist or racist thoughts in yourself or the desire to brutally dominate others. As long as you can stay with mere mental impulses and you do not act them out, you do not need to worry. On the contrary, you can try to channel such impulses into humour or into artistic projects, such as writing a dark novel or movie script.

However, if you notice that you pick more fights with your partner, punish your children too hard or try to dominate and humiliate other people, you should urgently try to seek help. As long as you still have the awareness that your behaviour is inappropriate, you are not really on the spectrum of personality disorders and you can benefit from therapy. In mild cases, the tantric relationship model can work wonders to help you by inducing liberating self-knowledge. While this work is not enjoyable, dissolving your narcissistic and out-of-control ego is the single most important spiritual task.

In the spiritual context, we use the term "ego" to refer to the pursuit of feigned superiority over others. Therefore, ego always takes place in and through relationships where the ego-driven person tries to use others to elevate themselves at the others' expense. This can happen, for example, through refusal to help, boasting, schadenfreude or by putting other people down in subtle or rude ways. Ego behaviour is also always accompanied by dishonesty and lies because the superiority that the ego strives for is never realistic but always faked. For example, the "super-nice" woman who is always friendlier than everyone else is not always so nice when you get to know her better. Or the great man who you thought was spiritually advanced turns out to be a controlling egomaniac once you are married to him. By contrast, you can recognise true spiritual development by the absence of desire for fake superiority and by the sincere and humble desire for mutual love and support.

Abuse of the kundalini power

People who have tendencies in the direction of personality disorders also have a greater willingness to abuse the kundalini process for their selfish purposes. I would love to say that this never happens but unfortunately, that is not the case. There are many examples of spiritual teachers with awakened kundalini who abuse these powers for their selfish ends. As already mentioned, Tibetan Buddhism speaks of the three poisons of the mind - hatred, greed and ignorance - and when these poisons are increased by the kundalini energy, it can look like this:

Hatred: Abuse of kundalini power for black magic; aggression against those who do not recognise one's own "enlightened status"; subtle or even brutal suppression and domination of one's family members and meditation students

Greed: Marketing of your supernatural abilities for financial gain; seduction and exploitation of spiritual students to satisfy sexual, financial and egotistical needs; attachment to bliss and aggression against anyone who disturbs this beautiful feeling

Ignorance: Fanciful ideas of being spiritual advanced; refusal to deal with one's own mistakes; delusional ideas of believing that one is the messiah.

Dealing with sexual problems

Like all other feelings and sensations, we also find that our sexuality is intensified during the kundalini process. On the positive side, this leads to stronger sexual feelings and orgasms but on the other hand, this will also intensify all of our sexual problems and hang-ups.

It can be said that the disharmony between the upper and lower chakras (love and power) can be seen most clearly in our sexuality. Even today, many women - despite their emancipation - have problems finding kind men sexually attractive. And many men agree that it is positive that women are successful in their jobs but at home, they should please continue to serve them (sexually) and not have too many demands. These pain-inflicting attitudes unfortunately do not stop once people become spiritual and often just take on a more veiled character. This is at least what I regularly see in my counselling practice. Many disputes in couple relationships are therefore a symptom of sexual desires that do not fit the needs of their hearts.

Even couples who have a successful relationship frequently notice that their sexual desires just do not harmonise with their spiritual ideals. The sexuality of many people is laced with aggressive, masochistic and promiscuous fantasies and creates confusion and shame. Moreover, the attempt to tame these "politically incorrect" desires through sexual tantric exercises, such as "slow sex", is not always easy because often all desire will simply dissipate.

All these problems cannot be fixed through a few simple tips and, indeed, even in the lives of many famous spiritual teachers, we can see again and again that they got into trouble through the topic of sex. In earlier centuries, attempts were made to erase the difficult issue of sexuality simply through celibacy but nowadays this is no longer seen as a solution as celibacy in itself leads to many new problems.

Therefore, I recommend to my clients to delay having sex at the beginning of a new relationship and to focus more on building a truly loving relationship with their future partner. When you are really in love with each other and have entered a committed relationship in which you have clarified all mutual expectations, it is time to celebrate this loving connection with the sexual union. In this way, you can ensure that love takes precedence over sex (and therefore also over power games) and have set the course of the relationship into a positive direction.

For the same reason, all sexual dysfunctions such as premature ejaculation or vaginismus are always much easier to resolve within a loving relationship. All attempts to "cure" these problems with a prostitute or a "tantric teacher" will exacerbate these problems by tearing the upper and lower chakras further apart instead of connecting them.

Tantric sex

When it comes to love-making, the tantric approach means that we are trying to connect the upper and lower chakras more closely with each other - just as in our entire development. This means that we try to combine our sexuality with as much love as possible. Real love means that we truly and deeply care for our partner and that we do everything possible to make them happy. This is certainly impossible in short-term sexual affairs or with strangers at a tantra workshop but only possible in a deeply committed partnership.

There are many books and guides on the topic of tantric sex, such as the programme of Mantak Chia that I myself practised for many years. Through my own experience and also through the reports of my clients, however, I have concluded that many of these exercises are too technical and complicated for most couples and tend to kill the sex drive instead of keeping it alive.

I recommend a simpler form of tantric sex: we do this by arousing each other in any form that we find pleasurable. During the sexual act with our partner, we pause now and then while looking into each other's eyes and focusing on the loving feelings between our hearts. We also say loving words to each other while the genital movements are only very gentle or have completely stopped. When the man feels that his erection is

196

diminishing, we can focus again on the sexual feelings in the abdomen and move in the way we find pleasurable. After a little while, we stop once again and focus on the feelings of love in the upper chakras. Through this back and forth between the upper and lower chakras, we gradually learn to connect love and (sexual) power more harmoniously and bring this harmony into other areas of our life.

Many tantric sex teachers advise restraining from having an orgasm. If someone enjoys doing this, they can do this, of course, but in my experience people - particularly younger people - will often find this frustrating. It also greatly contributes to the experience of mutual love when both partners show a willingness to fully satisfy their partner. This, of course, especially applies to men who should learn how their partner's body works and then bring her to orgasm every time they make love.

Fear of masturbation

In many books about kundalini coming from the East, there are dire warnings that men should not orgasm because otherwise, all sorts of horrible things could happen, such as "emptying the energy body" or the "inability to gain enlightenment". (Women are usually not even mentioned.) This, however, does not correspond with my experience - neither personally nor have I ever seen a client who has experienced negative consequences from having orgasms. One should not allow oneself, therefore, to be scared by these forms of out-dated advice. I see these Eastern ideas on the same level as the sexual suppression that was practised in our Christian culture not so long ago. As a culture, we have shaken off many of these shackles and I do not think it is wise to reintroduce them through the back door by adopting ancient Eastern ideas.

For young men in particular, it is very important that they regularly have orgasms when they suffer from kundalini symptoms. The orgasm works like a valve through which one can drain some of the pent-up energy and feel immediate relief. Orgasms are also very useful when suffering from insomnia and excessive sexual arousal.

Unfortunately, it is often those clients who suffer from sexual over-arousal who insist that their arousal will get worse if they masturbate. I cannot confirm that belief. Every single client who began to masturbate regularly had a significant reduction of sexual over-arousal along with a decrease of other kundalini symptoms. I, therefore, advise everyone to try this approach.

As I mentioned earlier, it is important not to use pornography while masturbating as these videos can cause many psychological problems and are morally wrong.

Sexual over- and under-arousal

During a kundalini awakening, people can experience periods of sexual over-arousal or a complete drying up of their libido. Someone who suffers from over-arousal should have sex with their partner or masturbate once a day as I described in the previous section. They can also relax the root chakra in the abdomen by visualising a flower opening up as I described in the anti-anxiety exercise in the fifth chapter. They should do this at least once a day for several minutes and when any over-excitement rises up in an unpleasant way.

Sexual under-arousal is much less of a problem. As long as there are no conflicts in your partnership and you are otherwise physically and psychologically healthy, it means that your entire life-force has been brought into your spirituality or other useful projects and that you have one big need less to satisfy. If your partner is unhappy with this development, you should try to continue having loving sex with them and focus more on the loving union than on genital pleasure. With a bit of goodwill from both sides, this solution is quite workable.

Dealing with unwanted sexual fantasies

Some of my clients suffer a lot from the fact that they can only come to orgasm through fantasies that they find disgusting or otherwise terrible. I had, for example, a female client who could only reach orgasm with her boyfriend if she imagined that he had sex with another woman. Once the sex was over, she was really angry at him and also felt very stupid. Many people have to imagine violent sexual acts to climax and then feel

198

disgusted and guilty about this afterwards.

I explain to my clients that, fundamentally, we cannot change our sexual preferences - just as we cannot make a gay person heterosexual or vice versa. It is therefore important to accept yourself as you are and neither suppress nor act out your unwanted sexual preferences. Instead, you should *manage* these desires.

In practice, managing these desires looks like this: when you masturbate or have sex with your partner, try to focus as long as possible on love and use your fantasies only just before the end to reach orgasm. As soon as you feel the orgasm coming, direct your mind back to the loving union with your partner. In this way, your sexual experience will always be very fulfilling.

Widening sexual desires

During a kundalini awakening, new and unfamiliar sexual impulses may emerge. For example, you can suddenly find gay or lesbian impulses in yourself even if you have been heterosexual all your life. You may even detect sadomasochistic tendencies in yourself or the desire to try group sex.

Some clients are terribly afraid about such developments because they believe that they have to act out these desires. But that is by no means the case. We are never forced to live out any of our fantasies. Instead, we can and should consciously decide how we want to conduct our relationships. If we proceed in this way, these impulses may sometimes be a positive addition to our sexual self, which can make life more exciting but not force us to do anything. Generally speaking, everything that intensifies our love for our partner is permitted and we should never do anything sexually that could hurt people.

Relationships with a spiritual teacher

Besides our partner, our most important relationships in the kundalini process are those with our spiritual teachers. There are always people who have the idea that they do not need guidance from others. This is similar to the idea that a child does not need to go to school but will learn everything that is needed in life all by themselves. This is, of course, an extreme attitude and does not represent the middle ground, which is so important for mastering the kundalini process. To become successful, it would be of great advantage to have the humility to learn from other people who are already further along this path than ourselves. People who reject this idea should be prepared for years of groping in the dark and having to admit in the end that, with a bit of guidance, they would have got there much faster.

On the other hand, some people are driven by fear to go to multiple energy-healers and spiritual teachers simultaneously, only to find that their symptoms become even more chaotic and harder to control. As I have previously described, many of my clients have an overly trusting attitude and do not always see the necessity for checking the qualifications of the people they go to for help. Instead, they believe that purely with their intuition they know whether someone has the necessary wisdom and integrity or not. Since I hear countless stories of people and their spiritual teachers in my work as a kundalini therapist, I would like to urgently point out that charlatans are extremely skilled people who can hide their true motivations to a degree that resembles an art form. It really is very unlikely to find a good spiritual teacher by the "love-at-first-sight" method. I will refrain from naming famous people here but everyone is free to search terms like "spiritual teacher" and "scandal" and read through the extremely high number of hits.

How can we deal with this dilemma? My advice is to check the teacher just as we would check a doctor, a lawyer, or even a tradesman whose services we want to use. Recommendations from friends who have become happier would be a good start. But we should also look for qualifications and find out who has given a potential teacher the permission to teach and keep clear of all self-proclaimed gurus. Would we let a self-proclaimed doctor, lawyer or electrician help us? In all likelihood, not. So why are we willing to take such a risk when it comes to the most precious things we possess – our mind and spiritual health?

If a spiritual teacher has undergone proper training and has been qualified by someone who has been qualified themselves, there is a degree of safety that we can never get from a self-proclaimed guru. Of course, even the best qualifications do not guarantee integrity. However, in my experience, the likelihood of such a person going on a megalomaniac ego trip is much smaller when they are surrounded by people who have a critical eye on them.

The second problem with self-proclaimed teachers is that they often just teach what has worked for themselves and they do not have an overview of different approaches to accommodate the different character-structures and needs of individuals. For example, a fearful teacher will usually over-emphasise self-soothing and teachings such as simply staying in the here-and-now and not worrying so much about the future. Unfortunately, for people with addictive tendencies, such instructions act as pure poison. These people need to be motivated to think as far as possible into the future so that they realise that their current addictive behaviour will have serious negative consequences. A spiritual teacher with a depressive past and low confidence will usually overemphasise the importance of self-love and techniques for self-assertion. This instruction, in turn, will act like poison for narcissistic people because they will simply use it to increase their egotism even more. These people need to be taught to love others more and self-cherish less. The following checklist can help you to choose a good spiritual teacher.

Checklist for finding a spiritual teacher

The teacher has undergone several years of intensive spiritual training and has been given permission to teach by a qualified person.

The teacher publicly speaks of their gratitude to their teachers.

The teacher clearly explains which spiritual system and lessons they follow. They also make it clear which are their own ideas and how they differ from traditional teachings.

The teacher behaves always and everywhere ethically and lovingly and does not show any tendencies towards addictive behaviour.

The teacher behaves exactly as he or she teaches.

There is no credible information about unethical behaviour or scandals around the teacher.

The teacher does not charge extremely high prices.

The most important foundation and goal of the teacher's spiritual teachings are love and compassion.

In our relationship with our spiritual teacher, it is important – just like in all other areas of our life – to find the middle ground between extreme devotion and total rejection of all spiritual authority. Therefore, we should always allow ourselves some critical scepticism yet at the same time accept that there are people who are higher in the spiritual hierarchy than we are and show them the appropriate respect.

A typical mistake made by many beginners is projecting unrealistic abilities onto a teacher and also giving them too much responsibility in their lives. I know several stories of people who asked their spiritual teachers if a certain relationship or job is "good" for them. They received confirmation from their teachers, went along with the advice and experienced huge disasters as a result. Other clients of mine held the belief that their teacher had the sole power to bring them well-being and happiness and that they themselves could do nothing. These are both forms of disempowerment that lead invariably to much suffering. At the other extreme, some people communicate with spiritual teachers only on an intellectual level and never really engage emotionally.

Therefore, it is all about finding the middle path where we can meet our spiritual teacher with respect and devotion but without giving away our power and healthy scepticism. The Buddha himself gave us the advice that we should always review all spiritual teachings and accept only those that help us. With this piece of advice, I would like to finish this book and encourage all my readers to check my teachings and only accept those pieces of advice that feel right and good to them.

Final words

I hope I have been able to provide extensive and detailed guidance for healing and eliminating all the many challenging symptoms of a kundalini awakening that I see in my counselling practice on a daily basis. I also hope that this book will be useful for therapists and physicians who may sometimes encounter clients and patients with these unusual symptoms in their own practices.

But no book about kundalini would be complete without the information about how to use this amazing energy for positive purposes. As I have already written several books about the positive use of kundalini power, I will limit myself here to a few brief references to these books.

The manifestation of wishes

Kundalini is a force that we can compare to money. Money in itself is neither good nor bad but can be used for positive or negative purposes. Through our increased kundalini power, we also have an increased capacity to consciously manifest our desires in all areas of our life. I have worked in this way for over thirty years and have succeeded more and more to manifest everything I wanted, starting with my relationships and health and then encompassing my work, my home and ultimately my spiritual desires. Everyone can copy me because I have described this technique in detail in my book *Advanced Manifesting*. It is of utmost importance to always formulate our desires such that they serve the highest good of all beings. Through this altruistic attitude, the fulfilment of our wishes also becomes an excellent means of our spiritual development.

Bliss and ecstasy

We all need something to eat, a roof over our head and physical safety. In addition, Buddhism teaches that we all just want to be happy. In its pure state, the kundalini energy is pure bliss. To experience this bliss, we must first apply the exercises described in this book in order to heal our most difficult problems. Bit by bit we should improve all areas of our life and should also use the methods that I have described. Once these basic requirements are met, we can turn the kundalini energy into pure bliss and continuously dwell in that state of mind. In Tibetan Buddhism, this method (which is actually not a real method) is called Dzogchen – the highest of their system of spiritual approaches and I have described it in my book *Spiritual Joy*.

Enlightenment or union with God

The ultimate goal of a kundalini awakening is to allow us to realise our divine nature (or Buddha nature or enlightenment) and to stabilise this state of mind. We can only reach this ultimate goal by emptying and purifying our entire unconscious mind as I have described in this book. Fundamentally, enlightenment can be achieved most easily simply through devotion to an enlightened being. Unfortunately, many people do not possess such deep devotion. Therefore, we can find countless techniques and meditation practices in Buddhism and in other religions to facilitate this development and make our enlightenment more likely. For this topic, I would recommend my books *Enlightenment Through the Path of Kundalini* and *Stairway to Heaven*.

About the author

Tara Springett has been in her own kundalini process for forty-three years and for the last ten years she has accompanied over a thousand clients in their journey of kundalini awakening. During these years, she has successfully helped her clients to alleviate and cure all of their kundalini symptoms. Tara`s websites contain positive feedback from hundreds of grateful clients who have experienced a great deal of relief from their problems by working with Tara.

Tara holds an MA in Education and has trained in Gestalt therapy, body awareness therapy and transpersonal therapy. Since 1988, Tara has worked as a drug addiction counsellor, a youth counsellor and a general psychotherapist.

Since 1986, Tara has practised daily Buddhist meditation and spent many weeks in individual and group retreats. In 1997, she received the empowerment of her Buddhist teacher, Rigdzin Shikpo, to teach meditation. In 2002, she was also asked by her Buddhist teacher, His Eminence Garchen Rinpoche, to teach.

Tara is a successful author of numerous self-help books that apply Buddhist wisdom to all areas of life: relationships, emotional issues, nutrition, wish fulfilment and others.

Tara lives in a retreat house in Devon, England with her soulmate and husband Nigel. Nigel is also a qualified counselling psychologist and had his kundalini awakening in 2006. Since 2018, he works under Tara`s guidance in her expanding kundalini therapy practice. Tara and Nigel focus on individual work with clients suffering from kundalini symptoms (via skype and phone). You can reach either of them on their website at the following address: www.taraspringett.com/contact.

www.taraspringett.com
www.kundalinisymptoms.com

Printed in Great Britain
by Amazon